THE AVENGER

THE RISE OF THE KINGDOM

THE AVENGER

THE RISE OF THE KINGDOM

ANITA ALEXANDER

Cover and Interior design by Sophie Pauli (www.annasophiadesign.com)

Reach us on the internet: www.revival-flame.org

ISBN 978-0-6485436-0-2

DEDICATED

TO CHRIST'S BELOVED ~ HIS BRIDE

ENDORSEMENTS

Anita Alexander is one of today's true prophetic voices who operates from a place of presence and intimacy with the Father, the true home of the prophetic. This book reflects the intimacy of sonship and honor of God's leading in all things by His Spirit, revealing a genuine prophetic & apostolic mantle being unveiled in the Body of Christ, preparing them for a massive outpouring of end time harvest. I recommend this raw and very real book birthed in the authors abandoned heart to you, as you also look to honor and value true sonship based on intimacy and union with and through the Holy Spirit.

Ian Johnson
His Amazing Glory Ministries
New Zealand
hagmian.com

Anita Alexander's "Avenger – Rise of the Kingdom" is perhaps one of the most relevant books of our time. As we stand at the threshold of the greatest move of God in history, Anita masterfully gives us one of the clearest descriptions of how it may unfold that I've ever read. Her accurate prophetic insights are profound and can only come from a deep, abiding walk with Christ. As I read this powerful manuscript, I was continually stirred that this is a must read for all those whose heart is completely fixed on Jesus and desiring to be ready for this extraordinary move of Glory.

Gary Beaton
Founder Transformation Glory
Author, Host, Prophetic Voice to the Nations
TransformationGlory.com

The Avenger what a word!!! You may wonder why I call this book a word, well that's because that's exactly what it is. It is a now word to the Church. The Avenger, is a plumbline word from the Lord to prepare His people to partner with Him in the greatest move of the Spirit of God upon the earth. As I read the pages of this amazing prophetic word, I wept and my heart burned with His fire as I heard His voice and heartbeat loudly.

Anita Alexander is not only a dear friend of mine but a prophet to the nations. She has carried this word for over 15 years. The depth, richness, anointing and clarity on this word testifies to her stewardship of allowing this word to germinate within her in intimacy with the Lord.

The Avenger is a game changer. A message released in purity, without mixture and a call to worship Jesus in Spirit and in truth. There is rich impartation contained in the words, there's a breaker anointing in the pages, it's a major key in the spirit to bring forth a great unlocking. It's a line in the sand. It's an invitation from the Lord to total abandonment and surrender to His ways and to partner with Him in this new day to see Him move in ways we have never imagined!!

The Avenger is in many ways a divine road map and a word you will refer to time and time again as we move into this new era!

Lana Vawser
Author, Speaker, Prophetic Voice
Queensland, Australia
lanavawser.com

Anita Alexander is a powerful prophetic voice who desires to see the Church as she is intended for her Beloved. Her book, The Avenger, is full of prophetic insight and a clarion call to return back to the Lord and to the heart of the Father. As I read this book, I found myself shouting an "Amen" to the call.

Dawn Hill
Writer & Blogger, Lovesick Scribe
Virginia, USA
lovesickscribe.com

The LORD is roaring out of Zion choosing to reveal Himself through His messengers whom He cloaks with a fire of zealous and jealous love.

Anita is such a messenger who comes in The Spirit of Elijah to awaken and prepare a people for the coming of Jesus. In the first chapters, Anita unlocks what this "coming" looks like and how to prepare for and be a partner with Him in this "coming".

Bold and unapologetic, she identifies the subtle and deceptive mixture of idols that have crept in to the Church, a tool of satan to subdue the Church into a slumber and complacency. Through prophetic encounters, dreams and visions, she identifies the spirits which war against the church and against individuals to keep them bound and immobile. She sounds the alarm of the urgency of the hour calling for a turning away from the "consumables", the added extras (idols) in the Church that have shrouded the simplicity and power of the truth of the gospel.

The book is written in an easy to read conversational style with wonderful scriptural prophetic application to our day and time. For those who are not familiar with the prophetic, Anita demonstrates how God speaks through dreams, visions and encounters to give warning, strategy and directions to His people as she relates her experiences and what The LORD is saying through her experiences to the Church today.

This is a book for church leaders. This is a book for "the congregation". Anyone who calls themselves by the name of the Lord should read this book. It is a call out of a form of religion into the reality of a relationship with a Living Lord, The King of The Universe.

"Without a vision, the people perish (cast off restraint/righteousness)" Proverbs 29:18. "Believe the prophets and you will live". 2 Chronicles 20:20. How we need vision in this hour, when confusion and chaos accelerate in the nations. How we need to hear the voice of God.

Anita is a voice for the hour. The message is urgent. The time is short. Her message, "Wake up and live".

Vivienne Docherty,
Prophetic Voice/Intercessor
Brisbane, Australia

The AVENGER is a prophetic message to the Church revealing the urgency of the hour to leaders and the Body of Christ of the Lords desire for His bride to be made ready and the divine strategy on how to partner with Him in all He wants to establish. Before even starting this book, the Lord spoke to me and told me it was a "Kingdom Key" which excited me before I even began reading! After completing it I can indeed see how this book is a Kingdom key to the Body of Christ in this significant time in history. It unlocks and reveals the times and seasons of God, and is a call to individuals and the body of Christ to awaken to the hour, arise into the fullness of all the Lord has purchased for us, and partner with Him to see His Kingdom advance.

Your hope will rise up as you read of Jesus your Avenger who has come to bring recompense and empower His people to overcome. The Lord is preparing His people for His arrival as the King of Glory, and this book is a key that outlines the preparation that must take place.

You will be given revelation on the need for the dismantling of that which is not in alignment with the heart and ways of God, the need to take up a Kingdom mindset and the power in allowing the Holy Spirit to move with freedom. You will be stirred to respond and passionately pursue His presence, be led by His Spirit, walk in your identity and authority in Christ and make way for the King of Glory.

This book is a strategic tool in the hands of intercessors, a prophetic message on the times and seasons of God and a declaration of all the Lord wants to bring forth. It is a message to the leadership of the church to allow the Spirit to move with freedom and a call to the Body of Christ to walk in the ways, love and power of God, align with the heart of God, be led by the Spirit and live to see Jesus glorified.

Katie Barker
Bring the Fire Ministries
Gold Coast, Australia
bringthefireministries.com
katiebarker.com

Throughout the centuries, at appointed times in history, God has raised up prophetic voices with a clarion call to contend against the tides of the enemy. A voice that calls His people to repentance, revival, and reformation. Anita Alexander is one of such voices, and now is the appointed time!

Her book the Avenger, the Rise of the Kingdom, serves as a blueprint to establish God's mandate on the earth today. Those who have an ear, let them hear what the Spirit says to the churches.

Matthew Russell, World for Christ,
Gold Coast, Australia
worldforchrist.net

I am blown away by the prophetic timing of this book. This is definitely a now word to the Body of Christ, especially strategic in this new era. Anita would have to be one of the most humble women of God I have met, balanced with truth and a genuine love for the King and His people. Get ready to see the Lord avenge you, pursue you and restore double for all your loss. The King of Glory is coming in indeed! This book will break you into the new. Now is the time…

Natalia Russell, World for Christ,
Gold Coast, Australia
worldforchrist.net

Anita and I have a friendship truly ordained of God. Through the years, we have spent countless hours analysing, unpacking, inspiring and affirming the move of God in each of our hearts; all with joy, laughter, light bulb moments and tears. The call of God upon Anita is to declare the Living Word of Truth that discerns and divides. The beautiful balance of this woman, is that she is love without judgement through and through, yet completely uncompromising in her call to challenge His bride to get "free" and get "ready", to surrender, align and burn for His glory in the earth.

Louise Nuss, Worship Pastor, Gold Coast, Australia

ACKNOWLEDGMENTS

To my husband Sasha, my greatest encourager and supporter, I am so grateful for how you continued to champion me throughout the many diverse seasons I have walked in birthing this book. Thank you for believing in me and honouring so well the call of God on my life. Thank you for all the "practical help" that you have given me to help shoulder my responsibilities in our family and ministry in order to achieve all my deadlines for the release of this book into the hands of the Body of Christ in this hour. To my kids, you also have sown into this book by sacrificing time with me, when in the final birthing stages, I had to "go away and be with the Lord to write". Thank you my precious pups. To my dear mother, thank you for your "practical help", encouragement and prayers.

To my dearest friends Angelique, Melissa, Lana, Louise and Katie, for the roles you have all played in being strategic instruments in the hand of the Lord as a voice in my life through the process of writing this book. I am so grateful to the Lord for the rich friendships we have and for how you love and invest into my life so intentionally. Thank you for listening, encouraging me and at times jolting me into action with direct unapologetic words of instruction from the Lord. Friends like you I wish for everyone.

A special thank you to dearest Yolande for her hours and hours of work assisting me with bringing this book into a finished product. You are a gem and are so appreciated for all the arduous hours of editing, researching publications, administration and being so invested in this project. To Dawn, thank you for assisting with the editing process and being that extra eye.

Finally, to Sophie, your outstanding cover and interior design, bringing to a reality and representing through picture, the story within the pages of this book.

CONTENTS

INTRODUCTION

When the Lord spoke to me in 2005 to write a book about my vision and encounter with the Lion of Judah in 2003, I never expected it to become a fourteen-year long journey. A fourteen-year journey of the Lord building a story in my heart to deliver to the church, to prepare her for the times to come. Encounters, dreams, visions, fire, refining, travail, valleys and vast wilderness were intricately woven into these fourteen years of my life birthing this message.

When I surrendered my life completely to Christ as a teenager, I was filled with an inconsumable passion for my King of Glory. In the following years, my passion for Him overflowed into a passion for His beloved, His bride, His Church, to whom He makes Himself known with relentless love. This passion for His beloved caused me to come to another place of surrender. A surrender to His call of being His mouthpiece, proclaiming His furious love which is stronger than death, calling forth an overcoming generation of true LOVERS OF GOD

Yes, the surrender to this call has come at a great cost, but I would pay it over and over again, even to play a small part in what matters to Him the most. That is His beloved burning with her first love, unspotted from the world, representing Him in honor, bringing glory to His name and rising in the fullness of all she has been granted access to through Christ and His eternal glory.

This message in this book is a call of His love to His bride, His beloved, to enter the mandate of heaven on earth. Those of you who read this book, know it is not by chance that you have come across this message. You are loved, pursued, and your Beloved is drawing you, deeper and higher, to run after Him.

Much Love in Christ our Beloved,

Anita Alexander

Chapter 1

THE RISE OF THE KINGDOM

In the winter of 2013 in a time of prayer and seeking the Lord's heart, I saw a vision of Jesus riding upon a horse coming out of heaven, with a sword in His hand. The full expression of His face announced urgency, passion, might, fury, justice and triumph. He was coming to encounter His people and He was purposeful in His mission. As I was beholding Him in this vision, He announced in my Spirit,

"Tell My people I am coming as the "AVENGER".

Immediately, I knew this meant war and victory all at the same time. As He revealed himself to me in this vision as the Avenger, I knew that it meant He was coming to make wrongs right, to restore, redeem, recover, repay and reconcile. I knew in my spirit He was coming in Victory, Power and Might, and just when His people were feeling deserted, defeated and cheated, the Lord wanted to announce to His people, He had not forgotten them and was about to avenge their cause, turn the tables and "show up" in unprecedented ways, displaying His glory and wonder.

This vision set me on course for a treasure hunt as most of my prophetic encounters do. "I must discover this Avenger", I thought, "I must discover Him throughout scripture as this man of war who simultaneously reflects love for His people but fury toward the enemy." And so, as I began the journey of discovering Him as the Avenger throughout scripture, I soon came to realise that this "Avenger", Jesus, our Beloved, is unveiled in Psalm 24 as the King of Glory. It was this mystery revealed, that unlocked a multitude of meaning behind the simple phrase He spoke to me; *"Tell them I am coming as the AVENGER"*. This Avenger is in fact the KING OF ALL KINGS. The KING OF GLORY. The Lion of the Tribe of Judah who has triumphed! (Revelation 3:5).

I began to see how Psalm 24 lays out a *precedent* for the King of Glory to "come in" and the part *we* play in partnering with Him. I saw the "way" that needed to be "prepared". I saw the role of government in the Church and how there must be a correct positioning to "make way" for our King of Glory to come.

The Lord showed me how a shift in government must take place within the current governing structure in the Body of Christ, to make room or make way for the Lord to be ushered in and display and manifest Himself as the King of Glory. For the King of Glory to "come in" is referring to His government, (which is the power and authority of heaven), His Kingdom, His rulership being established on this earth. When this takes place, wrongs are made right, justice is executed, and righteousness prevails.

VISION ~WAVES OF REVIVAL

Whatever did He mean by that phrase, *"I am coming"*? As I searched throughout scripture, I discovered that whenever the Lord says He is "coming", it simply means He is going to "appear", to "show up", to "manifest Himself". We see throughout history the Lord has "appeared", or "manifested himself" through different waves of revivals or awakenings. These revivals are in fact the Lord "appearing" or "coming" to His people. These "appearances" or "moves of God", always bring His people into a deeper understanding of *who He is,* consequently restoring a deeper knowledge and understanding of *who they are,* unlocking and unveiling greater mysteries of the Kingdom not yet given, or, restoring truths lost by previous generations.

In 1999 in a time of intercession, I saw a vision of waves on the ocean. The Lord explained to me how He moves by His Spirit as waves of glory upon His body, which reveals different aspects of His person in order to "prepare" a people ready for the Lord. In this vision, I saw waves of different colours all representing different anointings and revelations of the Kingdom that were to be poured out upon His beloved in the coming years. There were waves of blue symbolising the prophetic move and waves of gold symbolising the glory. I then saw a wave of red which I knew was a wave of fire. Next I saw a wave of purple which I knew symbolised the miraculous. In this wave of the miraculous came the fear of the Lord, and as the Spirit of the Lord moved through His people in miracles causing the impossible to be made possible, a sense of great awe fell amongst the people.

Then I heard the Lord say to me,

> *"Look at this last wave, it will be the last wave of My Spirit upon the earth."*

As I stood and looked there was no wave rising on the ocean; it was dead calm. This suggested to me that this would be different somehow to the past waves or moves of God that I saw move as a wave does, a coming then a going. However, as I looked, I saw the vast water dead calm. There was neither movement nor suggestion of a coming and a going, but rather something that would remain. As I looked at the water, the reflection from the sun upon the water was blinding. I asked the Lord, *"What is this wave?"* Immediately I heard the scripture of Psalm 37:6:

> *And He will make your uprightness and right standing with God **go forth as the light**, and your justice and right as the **[shining sun of] the noonday** (emphasis added).*

5

Note it says **He** will make. That's what these waves of revival do, *He makes ready His bride*. He makes ready His people by moving upon them in different expressions of His Spirit. All these previous waves were preparing His people for the last one.

THE LAST WAVE ~ THE MANIFESTATION OF THE SONS OF GOD

This last wave I saw in the vision is what I believe all creation is groaning and crying out for. This is the manifestation or the "revealing" of the sons of God, His glorious bride radiating the reflection of the Son of Righteousness shining as the "noonday" sun. Note that noon is at twelve o'clock. Twelve signifies divine government. This last wave is the glory of the Lord upon His people walking in the divine government of heaven. This is where heaven meets earth through the sons of God. Righteousness and justice will be the mark of this Kingdom Government, and it will bring alignment and order to the chaos and rebellion on this earth. This government will subdue and rule in justice and righteousness, causing wrongs to be made right and that which is lawless to be in subjection to the authority of the Lord Jesus Christ.

Malachi 4:2 explains that the Sun of Righteousness will arise on His people with healing in His wings and His beams, causing them to be released like calves released from the stall leaping for joy. Then verse 3 explains the direct result of this move upon His people,

> *You shall tread down the lawless and wicked, for they shall be ashes under the soles of your feet in that day I shall do this, says the Lord of hosts.*

Notice here *who* signs off on this declaration. He signs off as the "Lord of Hosts". That is the King of Glory, the Avenger, we see in Psalm 24. This speaks of the rule of Kingdom Government on the earth *through* His people. This is a people first avenged by the Lord, healed and set free (Malachi 4:2) then released to set others free (*tread down the lawless and the wicked becoming ashes under the soles of their feet*) (verse 3).

When the KING OF GLORY comes in, He not only shows Himself strong on behalf of His people, but He causes His Kingdom to operate *through* His people.

KEYS OF THE KINGDOM ~ GOVERNMENTAL DOMINION

Now do not be mistaken my friends, as Ephesians 6:12 explains our wrestle and war is not with flesh and blood. This means our enemy is not humanity but rather principalities and powers and rulers of darkness in heavenly places. These are the lawless and the wicked referenced in Malachi 4.

So how will we "tread down the lawless and the wicked" and how do they become "ashes under the soles of our feet", if we are not fighting flesh and blood?

In Matthew 16:19, Jesus tells His disciples:

> *I will give you the keys of the kingdom of heaven; and whatever you bind (declare to be improper and unlawful) on earth must be what is already bound in heaven; and whatever you loose (declare lawful) on earth must be what is already loosed in heaven.*

These keys that the Lord said He would give His Church is the key of David revealed in Isaiah 22:22:

> *And the key of the house of David I will lay upon his shoulder; he shall open and no one shall shut, he shall shut and no one shall open.*

Keys represent authority and ownership. When Jesus said in Matthew 16:19 that He has given us the keys to the Kingdom, it means He has given us authority and ownership *of* the Kingdom. When you purchase your house or your car, you can't use or access them without keys. If you don't have keys, then you don't have ownership or access. Therefore, the keys of the Kingdom explained here are keys to the Kingdom of heaven. So, we see here that the Key of David that Jesus in fact gave His people is the ability to open and to close gates or access points on earth. We have access to the authority and dominion of the Kingdom of heaven, and we have authority to govern earth as it is in heaven.

In this same verse, Matthew 16:19, Jesus goes on to explain how to use them, and how to govern. We use these keys to close and to open by the declarations of our mouth in accordance to the Word of God.

> *For whatever you bind **(declare to be unlawful)** on earth must be what is already bound **(declared unlawful)** in heaven (emphasis added).*

The keys to the Kingdom are really our dominion on earth through our ***declaration***. The keys to the Kingdom open and close as His people declare the Word of the Lord from their mouth. He says you will declare what is unlawful, to those things that are unlawful in heaven.

This is what Malachi 4 explains as lawless. When Malachi 4:3 says that we *"shall tread upon the lawless and the wicked and they shall be ashes under the soles of your feet"*, it means that whatever is unlawful in heaven will be ashes under the souls of your feet, by the declaration of the Word of the Lord coming forth from your mouth.

Notice he says here it will be *ashes* under the soles of your feet? Let me ask, what causes ashes? The answer would be fire, would it not?

> *Is not my word like fire [that consumes all that cannot endure the test]? Says the Lord (Jeremiah 23:29a).*

What are those things that cannot stand the test? All things that are under the rulership and influence of the corruptible kingdom of the god of this world. Sickness, disease, poverty, destruction, hatred, violence, injustice etc. These are all examples of what is unlawful in heaven and thus lawless on earth, and when met with a people walking in the Kingdom Davidic government of heaven of righteousness and justice, they are made as ashes under the soles of their feet.

In prophetic language when something is under your feet it represents under your authority and you have the victory over it. As God's people open their mouths and decree the word of the Lord that is fire, those things that stand as their enemies that are unlawful in heaven, will be defeated and under their feet. Burned to a crisp, nothing but ashes!

Chapter 2

THE AVENGER

When I saw the vision of the Lord as the Avenger on the white horse with a sword in his hand (that I explained in the last chapter), it revealed a picture of war. It was a picture of a man of war, but in the same token a picture of one who is coming to fight for the one He loves and bring about complete victory.

THE MIGHTY MAN OF WAR

Who is this King of glory? The Lord strong and mighty, the Lord mighty in battle
(Psalm 24:8).

In this verse the King of Glory is referred to as *strong, mighty* and *mighty in battle*. In other words, He is a MIGHTY MAN OF WAR!

Verse 10 asks the question again,

> *Who is [He then] this King of Glory? The Lord of Hosts,*
> *He is this King of Glory.*

Meaning the Captain of the Army. Again, this speaks of WAR!

> *The Lord shall go forth as a mighty man, He shall stir up*
> *jealousy like a **man of war**: He shall cry, yea, **roar**; He shall*
> *prevail against His enemies*
> *(Isaiah 42:13 KJV emphasis added).*

When the Lord manifests as the Mighty Man of War – aka: The King of Glory; interestingly enough, the sound that is released upon His enemies is a roar. This is the sound that speaks of the all Triumphant One, The Lion of the Tribe of Judah who has overcome, who roars and prevails over His enemies! Did you know that *His* enemies are *your* enemies?

> *The Lion of the Tribe of Judah, the Root of David, has*
> *overcome and conquered!*
> *(Revelation 5:5 AMP).*

As the Lion of the Tribe of Judah roars over His people, this sound will be imparted into them and they will carry this same sound of victory. The Lord's people will walk in the roar of the Lion, they will resound a sound of justice, and recompense, giving birth to victory and righteousness.

LION OF JUDAH

In the spring of 2003, I was ministering in the USA in a series of revival meetings. During worship in one of the services, I had an encounter with the Lord. I saw the face of a lion appear before me and its mane was flowing with power. The expression on the lion's face was authority and might. As I beheld His face, I heard His voice so loud in my Spirit,

> **"My people have known me as the Lamb but they are yet to know me as the Lion".**

My whole being was trembling at His voice echoing within my spirit. He continued:

> **"They have known me as the Saviour, the Lamb that was slain, the One who paid the ultimate price for the forgiveness of their sins, who made a way for their eternal salvation, but, are yet to "know" me (experientially) as the Lion, the King of Glory, King of all Kings and Lord of all Lords, the all Victorious and Triumphant One. As they "know" me as the Lion, they will demonstrate and walk in the authority of the Lion - The King of Heaven and will execute My will on the earth."**

What struck me powerfully was the Lord's reference to "knowing" Him. He didn't use language like "seen" or "heard of". To "know" is very different than to "know about". To "know" someone is to become intimately acquainted with them. When Adam "knew" Eve, she became pregnant and bore Cain (Genesis 4:1). And so, I had this understanding when He was speaking to me, that His people have "known about" Him as the Lion of the tribe of Judah, by knowledge of scripture, but they are yet to "know" Him via *experience*.

The Lord is coming to encounter His people as the Lion. No longer are they going to know *about* this Lion, and merely talk *about* Him, but they will experience the thunder of His roar, causing that which can be shaken to shake, and they will see the effects and marks of the enemy that have been strongholds in their lives, cities and nations falling away and coming to nought (Hebrews 12:26-27).

As the Church "knows" Him as the Triumphant One who has overcome, she will conceive and birth a generation of overcomers who will usher in the King of Glory.

As I had this encounter with the Lord, I knew the Church was shifting into an Apostolic Government she had not yet walked in. As He was communicating this to me, I knew in my Spirit that He would first come *to* His Church and then He would move *through* His Church. He was coming to encounter His people in a display of might and power of the Kingdom they had yet known or experienced and consequently, they would then move and operate in this Kingdom realm here on the earth. They would then subdue nations and execute vengeance upon the enemy by the Spirit of the Lord.

CLOTHES OF VENGEANCE

As we just read, Psalm 24 unveils this King of Glory as a Mighty Man of War, mighty in battle. Isaiah 40:10 informs us that when the Lord comes to rule in "might", He comes with restitution (vengeance) and reward (recompense).

> *Behold, the Lord God will come with **might**, and His arm will rule for Him. Behold, His **reward** is with Him, and His **recompense** before Him (Isaiah 40:10).*

Therefore, this King of Glory is our Avenger, He is the Mighty One, the Man of War who repays, redeems and rewards.

> *For He [the Lord] put on righteousness like a coat of armour, And salvation like a helmet on His head; He put on garments of **vengeance** for clothing and covered Himself with zeal [and **great love for His people**] **as a cloak**. As their deeds deserve, so He will repay: Wrath to His adversaries,*

retribution to His enemies; To the islands and coastlands He will repay (Isaiah 59:17-18 AMP emphasis added).

The Lord clothes himself in vengeance and cloaks himself in the zealous love He has for His people. Love and vengeance are his garments. Love and vengeance are what He chooses to wear. This is not even speaking of armour. Although he does speak of righteousness and salvation as armour, clothing is something different.

Clothing speaks of identity. When I put on clothes, I express my identity in what I wear. My preferences in colour, in texture and in design are evident. Clothing refers to identity on display.

When the Lord "clothes" himself with vengeance and cloaks himself in zealous love, this displays who He is and what He is about. He is consumed with a zealous love for His people, and He is so intentional and focused in His pursuit of justice and recompense for those He loves.

Isaiah 59:17 paints a picture of our King as this man of war being a man of vengeance motivated by love. When the Lord is referred to as a man of war, it means He is going to war and in war there is battle. Why is He battling? For whom does He battle? He is fighting for *you*, His beloved. He is purposeful in seeing wrongs made right, justice given, and retribution paid. He is driven by a love that is as strong as death, a love that compelled Him to make every wrong right at the cross. It is a love so full of vengeance that He would pay the highest price to intercept a people who would accept that sacrifice from eternal damnation.

What does this vengeance look like?

In various dictionaries vengeance is referred to as: retributive justice, recompense and repayment.

This explanation shows us that vengeance is not only revenge, but it is recompense and repayment for the loss of the affliction from the enemy.

RETRIBUTION ~ BEAUTY FOR ASHES

To proclaim the acceptable year of the Lord [the year of His favour] and **the day of vengeance of our God,** *to comfort all who mourn, To grant [consolation and joy] to those who mourn in Zion- to give them an ornament (a garland or diadem) of* **beauty** *instead of ashes, the oil of joy instead of mourning, the garment of praise instead of a heavy, burdened, and failing spirit – that they may be called oaks of righteousness,[lofty, strong, and magnificent, distinguished for uprightness, justice, and right standing with God], the planting of the Lord, that He may be glorified (Isaiah 61:2-3 emphasis added).*

We see here in this scripture that after the Lord declares the day of vengeance, there is a "turning". When the Lord avenges, he *turns* the wrongs and makes them right. He replaces mourning with comfort and healing. He replaces sorrow with joy, ashes with beauty, oppression, depression and defeat with praise and shouts of victory!

When the Lord shows up as the Avenger, the destruction of the enemy that has marked His people's lives with ashes, He (By His Spirit – Isaiah 61:1), will not only heal that area but He will beautify it! He will *adorn* it and use it as a platform to display His glory.

According to the Strong's Concordance, the word *beauty* that is referred to in this passage of scripture in the Hebrew comes from a root word which can mean: to boast of oneself and to glorify.[1]

I was excited when I saw this because I see this as a picture of the Lord glorifying Himself in the very place the enemy has sought to mark your life by afflicting you with pain, sorrow, grief or destruction. He will turn that which the enemy meant for evil for good (*Genesis 50:20*).

Part of the Lord's retribution upon the enemy is turning what the enemy meant for evil into glory to His name!

> *The thief comes only in order to steal and kill and destroy.*
> *I came that they may have and enjoy life, and have it in*
> *abundance (to the full, till it overflows) (John 10:10).*

Where the devil has ripped you off and tried to destroy, kill and steal your life, steal your family, your mind, your finances, your years, your health, let it be known that the Lord is coming as the mighty one, the Mighty Man of War to recover and restore, to recompense and repay.

TWO FOLD RECOMPENSE

As noted previously, part of the meaning of the word vengeance is recompense. Another way of saying recompense is compensation.

The Lord pays compo. In Australia we have employment insurance called Workers Compensation. It is insurance for the employee in case of injury in the workplace, whereby the employee can claim and receive benefit if their injuries restrict them from working or returning to work. We Australian's love to shorten and abbreviate most words, and we refer to this insurance as "compo". As a common occurrence in most insurance claims, this insurance can occasionally be challenging to receive and is sometimes very restricted in its time frame of compensation. But when the Lord pays "compo", when He compensates you for loss, trauma, trouble and affliction, there are no restrictions. He is heartfelt in His compensation to you, and as we saw according to Isaiah 61:2-3, His compensation always outweighs the loss. He *doubles the blessing* for the trouble the enemy has caused. One of His wonderful job descriptions is Redeemer, Repairer of the breach. He always replaces mourning with joy and beauty instead of ashes.

Now is a season where God is taking vengeance upon the cause and effects of the enemy in His people's lives and is destroying that yoke of shame, reproach, disillusionment, and confusion. He has come as the Avenger to bring recompense in a double fold portion!

> *Instead* *of your former]* **shame** *you shall have a* **twofold** **recompense***; instead of dishonour and reproach [your people] shall* **rejoice** *in their* **portion***. Therefore, in their land they shall possess double [what they had forfeited]; everlasting joy shall be theirs (Isaiah 61:7 emphasis added).*

Let's take a moment and do a little word study on this scripture.

The word *instead* defines as: in the place of, or to replace one thing with something else.

The Lord is clearly saying here, that *in replace of* shame, *in replace of* dishonour and reproach*,* He will give a *twofold recompense* and He will cause you to inherit *double* of what was originally promised to you. In other words, when God recompenses you, you are better off than what you would have been before your trouble and affliction.

Let's look at the word *shame*. According to the Strong's Concordance *shame* in the Hebrew is *bo-sheth;* this translates: shame (the feeling and the condition, as well as its cause) – confusion.[2]

It is from a root word *boosh,* which translates as: pale – (which is defined as: to decrease in relative importance), dishonor, be disappointed or delayed, to be confounded (various dictionaries explain confounded as meaning to be confused, circumstances to be thrown into disarray and disorder, I call it being blindsided by the enemy), become dry, delay or be long.[3]

Shame is explained in various dictionary meanings as: A painful emotion caused by a strong sense of guilt, embarrassment, unworthiness, or disgrace (disapproval, disrespect, discredit), dishonor, condemnation, disappointment.

Wow! We can see there is a whole lot of meaning to that word shame! When you look in the Hebrew it is very expanded and revealing. Seeing this word now in this light breaks open the meaning of the scripture on a deeper level.

Sometimes things happen in our lives that we didn't expect. We have no understanding of how or why God even allowed it to happen. This is the very meaning of being *confounded*, (which is one of the meanings of the word shame). Further, it means to be *confused* and as you can see previously noted is also one of the meanings of shame.

When we go through situations and circumstances like this in our lives, when we feel blindsided by the enemy, it tests our belief in God to the very core. It can leave us feeling a sense of confusion in what we really believe. These experiences however can cause a shaking and uprooting of false concepts and beliefs and re-establish in us a deeper, stronger faith in the Lord. In these trying times of unexpected situations and trials, we can experience a sense of confusion and deep disappointment, despair, loss or regret which can overwhelm us and cause us to sink into deep depression. This is when we truly feel like our light is being snuffed out. BUT, God is faithful and just! He will not let us endure beyond what we can handle without providing a "way" out, (I Corinthians 10:13). He, Jesus, is that "way" amen (John 14:6, Revelation 1:8).

The Lord's promise to us in Isaiah 61:7 is this; in the place of your shame, dishonour and reproach, I am giving you *joy* and *inheritance* in a *"two-fold measure"*! Two-fold simply means twice as much!

An old Pentecostal saying is, "God will give you double for your trouble", and here we see this is scripturally accurate. When the Lord recompenses and compensates, He does so in a two-fold measure. His justice is not only fair, but it is good. Scripture clearly states here in black and white, when He avenges our cause, He makes sure we are positioned better than what we would have been if we hadn't suffered the affliction.

Let's continue in our word study in this passage of scripture. The next word I want to look at is the word *rejoice*. The Hebrew meaning according to Strong's Concordance is *ranan;* which means to shout, aloud, for joy, to sing for joy, to triumph.[4]

Hold that thought while we continue and look at the word *possess.* According to Strong's Concordance this word in the Hebrew is *yarash,* this means: to occupy by driving out previous tenants and possessing in their place, to seize, to rob, to inherit, to expel, to impoverish, to ruin, cast out, consume, destroy, without fail, possess, take possession, seize upon, succeed utterly.[5]

As I read this, I feel like doing laps around my room in excitement. Did you see what I saw? This is powerful folks!

This passage from Isaiah 61:2 where the vengeance of God is released, right through to verse 7 where recompense is spelled out, can be summed up literally in one sentence:

When the Lord comes as the Mighty Man, He empowers His people to overcome!

Can you see this? He first comes and "turns". He gives comfort for mourning, beauty instead of ashes, oil of joy for mourning and praise in place of depression and heaviness. Then He empowers and anoints His people for victory in the battle and He causes them to take what is rightfully theirs. They will *rejoice* in their *portion* by the Spirit of the Lord manifesting upon them as the victor. Then they drive out the enemy, destroy him, impoverish his quest on their lives and without fail, utterly succeed in possessing what is rightfully theirs.

Therefore, this is how I read Isaiah 61:7 after we expounded it in the Hebrew:

> *Instead of experiencing shame, guilt, embarrassment, unworthiness, disgrace – (disapproval, disrespect, discredit), dishonor, and a sense of unimportance and condemnation,*

and instead of being disappointed and confused to the point of nearly giving up by delayed promises and confounded by circumstances which threw your life into disarray and disorder, I the Lord will compensate you for loss and repay you with twice as much honor, credibility, approval, acceptance, hope, vision, restoration, peace, joy and fulfillment as you would have had if you had not experienced this shame! You will be victorious over the enemy that is occupying the inheritance that I have given you and you will shout aloud with a great shout as you drive out, consume, destroy and expel your enemy. You shall impoverish his presence and utterly succeed when you seize upon, take possession of and inherit what I have promised you. You shall go in, receive and retrieve a double portion of the original promise and everlasting joy will be yours!

Don't you just LOVE IT!

That is what it looks like when the Lord manifests as the Avenger and moves upon His people as the Victor. Let me say it again, your enemies are His enemies. Even those enemies that have been longstanding for generations, the Lord is coming as the Mighty Man of War laying the axe to the root, redeeming and turning the tables on cycles of death, destruction, affliction, shame and reproach.

As the Lord engages His people in this hour as the Mighty Man of War, the Avenger, the Lion of the Tribe of Judah, He is ushering His Church into the greatest shift and awakening she has ever encountered, causing her to rise up as the overcoming bride He will return to receive.

THE DAY OF VENGEANCE

All throughout scripture, vengeance is commonly referred to in alignment with times and seasons language. There is a *day* of retribution, a *time* for pay back and a *season* of recompense.

> The Lord laughs at [the wicked], for He sees that their own
> **day** [of defeat] is coming
> (Psalm 37:13 emphasis added).

> For the Lord has a **day** of **vengeance** a **year** of **recompense**
> for the cause of Zion
> (Isaiah 34:8 emphasis added).

> To proclaim the acceptable year of the Lord [the year of
> His favour] and the **day** of **vengeance** of our God
> (Isaiah 61:2-3 emphasis added).

In these scriptures above, we see the Lord's vengeance being noted as a "day". It is a *times* word, referring to a *moment* or *season*. This word describes an "appointment" of His vengeance.

In this life we can suffer injustice, affliction and destruction and it seems that the enemy has gotten away with everything. "Where is justice? How could this happen? When will I see justice or recompense?", are questions we can often find ourselves asking from time to time. Know that there is an appointed time for vengeance and justice.

We are entering that "Day" of vengeance as a generation is being prepared of the Lord to "make way" for the King of Glory to "come in". Wrongs are being made right, recovery, recompense, justice and reward taking place as the Lord the Avenger shows Himself strong on behalf of His people and avenges their cause. He truly is our knight in shining armour.

OUR KNIGHT IN SHINING ARMOUR

This King of Glory, the Avenger, is desperately seeking to show himself strong on behalf of His people.

> *For the eyes of the Lord run to and fro throughout the whole earth to show **Himself strong** in behalf of those **whose hearts are blameless** toward Him*
> *(11 Chronicles 16:9 emphasis added).*

The Lord is going to and fro, to and fro, to and fro, seeking, looking, seeking, looking throughout the *whole earth* to see *who* He can be *strong* for, *who* He can *show up* for, *who* He can *fight* for. This scripture excites my heart because when we look into the Hebrew meaning in the Strong's Concordance, it unveils the Lord as the Strong Man, the One who fights for us.

To *show Himself strong* in the Hebrew according to Strong's Concordance is *Chazaq*. Summarized, this means: to help, repair, fortify, conquer, prevail, mighty, recover, ***play the man*** and ***to behave valiantly.***[6]

Can you see in these meanings the Lord is wanting to "play the man" in our lives and be the "valiant" one for us? He wants to be our knight in shining armour, the one who recovers, helps, conquers and prevails for us. He wants to "BE THE MAN"! In fact, He is looking fervently for a life He can display Himself in this manner. Where He can show forth victory, might, recompense and deliverance. He is actively *seeking* out to and fro throughout the whole earth for someone He can show Himself strong to on their behalf. He *seeks* to be the knight in shining armour and act valiantly on behalf of His beloved. Someone who will *let* Him "play the man", deliver, rescue and cause him or her to prevail and conquer. This is the King of Glory, the man of war, who seeks to take vengeance for the cause of His beloved.

MIGHTY FOR THE SURRENDERED

This verse in 11 Chronicles 16:9, emphasises how the Lord seeks such a person, even to the ends of the earth. I thought to myself, "surely you don't have to look very far to see if there is someone in need who you can show yourself valiantly to and rescue, Lord!" But then I saw it, yes, I read the rest of the verse. I noticed there is a *type* of person that the Lord wants to engage with to "show Himself strong". It's not just anyone in trouble. Notice it says to "*a heart that is blameless before him*".

The Hebrew meaning of a *heart that is blameless* according to Strong's Concordance is *shalem,* which means: peaceable, ***made ready*.**[7]

When I read this meaning, it was like a fire cracker went off in my heart! I saw it! This is referring to a heart that must be "made ready" and positioned for the Lord to "show Himself strong". The Lord is coming to His people as the Mighty Man of War, the King of Glory, the Lord strong and mighty, but the "way" needs to be prepared and made ready!

This is what Psalm 24 verse 7 and 9 refers to when it says,

> *Lift up your heads oh ye gates, lift them up you age abiding doors,* ***that*** *the King of Glory* ***may come in*** *(emphasis added).*

The word *that* refers to the connotation that *something must take place in order for something else to take place.* A *way* needs to be made in order for Him to "come in".

We see this principle again and again throughout scripture, but the main example would be where the Lord sent John the Baptist in the spirit and power of Elijah to "prepare" or "make ready" the *way* of the Lord (Luke 1:17).

The *way* refers to the hearts of men and women being positioned to receive the weight of His coming. When the heart is "made ready" as it is put in this verse in 2 Chronicles 16:9, it is humble, surrendered and aligned under His mighty hand, ready to receive the Might of the Lord.

1 Peter 5:6 NKJV says:

> *Humble yourself under the **mighty hand** of God that He*
> *may exalt you in due time (emphasis added).*

We see here the position that is needed for the mighty hand of God to move. For it was by His *mighty* outstretched hand that the Lord delivered the children of Israel out of their slavery in Egypt (Exodus 6:6). The *mighty* hand or the outstretched arm of the Lord is a phrase in Judaic tradition representing God's use of His power on behalf of the Jews. When the Lord says humble yourself under the "Mighty Hand of God", it means submit, surrender and yield to His ability to move for you. It is a yielding to His ability to perform for you that which you cannot do for yourself. He wants to "play the man" and exalt us. That means He wants to perform, be strong for us and bring us to where we need to be. However, we need to clearly position ourselves in humility for Him to move mightily on our behalf. It is humility. For only a heart that is prepared can encounter Him when he comes. That is why the Lord is looking to and fro for a heart that has been positioned for Him to come as the King of Glory, the Lord Strong and Mighty. Because when the King of Glory shows up, there is also a *weight* that comes with it.

THE WEIGHT OF HIS COMING

Who is this King of glory? (Psalm 24:8a)

The word *glory* in the Hebrew according to Strong's Concordance is *kabod*. It means: weight, splendour, copiousness, glorious.[8]

His reward is weighty. It's not just lollipops. When the Lord comes with pay back, recompense and reward, it carries significant *weight*. Only a prepared heart can partner with that type of splendour.

For the "King of Glory" to show up, significant preparation must take place. If a nation were to host a king, the government of that nation would spend a significant amount of time preparing for his coming. And so, it is with us, the Lord is greatly aligning, and preparing His people for His arrival as the King of Glory.

The first time Jesus came as the Lamb, the *way* needed to be prepared. This time He is coming as the Lion, and thus again the *way* needs to be prepared and made ready.

Chapter 3

MAKE WAY FOR THE KING OF GLORY

When the Lord reveals to His prophets *how* He desires to move, it is for the intent and purpose of preparing the way and making ready His people. The Lord says He doesn't do anything unless He reveals it to His prophets first (Amos 3:7). Why is that? Because they intercede and birth the Word in the earth. It is the people of God's responsibility to adhere to the Word, agree and align themselves with the Word and be like Mary and say, *"Be unto me according to thy word"* (Luke 1:38 KJV). The Lord has precedents in how things must be aligned in order for Him to move. Psalm 24 is an expository of "how" the Lord desires to manifest Himself in our generation and it is a planned precedent.

PREPARATION FOR THE COMING KING

I indeed baptize you with water unto repentance, but He who is coming after me is mightier than I, whose sandals I am not worthy to carry. He will baptize you with the Holy Spirit and Fire (Matthew 3:11 NKJV).

John was speaking of a coming glory the earth had never seen or experienced. This baptism of the Holy Spirit and fire was a glory about to be revealed, a "coming" of the Lord that indeed required preparation. That preparation was repentance.

We then see John *revealing* or *unveiling* **how** the Lord was going to meet with His people, as the Lamb of God.

The next day John saw Jesus coming toward him and said, "Behold! The Lamb of God who takes away the sin of the world! This is He of whom I said, 'After me comes a Man who is preferred before me, for He was before me.' I did not know Him; but that He should be revealed to Israel, therefore I came baptizing with water"
(John 1:29-31 NKJV).

When John the Baptist declared, *"Behold the Lamb of God who takes away the sins of the world"*, it was like he literally took off the veil and revealed who He was and why He came. And so, in a likewise manner, the role of the prophetic voice is to *proclaim* and *reveal* who He is and why He has come.

We are now in another season of preparation for He is about to come again. He is coming as the Avenger, The Lord Strong and Mighty, The Lord Mighty in Battle, The Lord of Hosts, the all victorious Lion of Judah, the King of Glory. To avenge the cause of Zion, to bring recompense and justice, making every wrong right, to bring a people into walking in the overcoming face of the Lion.

THE SPIRIT AND POWER OF ELIJAH ~ STRATEGY OF PREPARATION

Let's for a moment revisit Isaiah 40:10:

> *Behold, the Lord God will come with might, and His arm will rule for Him. Behold, His reward is with Him, and His recompense **before** Him (emphasis added).*

We see here in this verse, something very interesting. When the Lord comes as the mighty man to rule as the King, notice it says that recompense goes *before* Him. Come with me now, as we embark on a journey looking into the spirit of Elijah, discovering that this "way making" anointing, that prepares and aligns hearts, is in fact a spirit of reconciliation and restoration, that "goes before" our coming King.

In Malachi 3:1, the Lord said that He would send His messenger to prepare the way *before* Him. Luke 1:17 reveals that this messenger was indeed John the Baptist who came in the spirit of Elijah, to "prepare the way*" before* Him. As noted in the previous chapter the "*way*", He is referring to is the heart. We see this was the strategy of the Lord, sending messengers to proclaim His Word to align the hearts of men in order to receive that which was promised. This strategy has not changed.

Jesus was even quoted as saying in Matt 17:11-12a AMP:

> *Elijah is coming and will restore all things; but I say to you Elijah has come already.*

If we look at this, it doesn't seem to make sense. On one hand Jesus is saying Elijah is coming, but then He is saying He has already come. May I suggest to you that it is indeed both. Elijah *is* coming, meaning the spirit of Elijah continues to manifest through His prophets continually preparing the way for the Lord's coming, (both seasonal and in the timeline of the ages), but indeed the very specific instance of preparing the way for Messiah's manifestation on earth had happened in and through John the Baptist. Hence Elijah is coming – the continued message of the prophets and Elijah has come – in the manifestation of John the Baptist at that moment in time.

THE MANTLE OF CAMEL'S HAIR ~ THE ANOINTING TO TURN HEARTS

As John the Baptist was the messenger described in Malachi 3 who came in the spirit and power of Elijah to prepare the way before the Lord, it is interesting to note John's attire was camel's hair like that of Elijah (2 kings 1:8, Matthew 3:4).

The primitive Hebrew root meaning of the word *camel* according to the Strong's Concordance is: to deal bountifully with, to requite, to *recompense* and to *reward*.[1]

This mantle worn by Elijah and John the Baptist is a symbol of reconciliation and restoration, turning the hearts of the fathers to the children and the children to the fathers (Luke 1:17, Malachi 4:5). The spirit and power of Elijah is an anointing of *reconciliation*, *restoration* and *repentance* (which is simply "turning" one's back on the world and turning it towards the Lord).

For even as John the Baptist went in the spirit and power of Elijah and was a voice to cause a return of the lost sheep of Israel, so that same mantle of the spirit of Elijah is being released in this hour, infiltrating the *world* and the *Church* to cause a great return of the lost and the prodigal back to the heart of the Father.

And he will [himself] go before Him in the spirit and power of Elijah, to turn back the hearts of the fathers to the children, and the disobedient and incredulous and unpersuadable to the wisdom of the upright [which is the knowledge and holy love of the will of God] – in order to make ready for the Lord a people [perfectly] prepared [in spirit, adjusted and disposed and placed in the right moral state] (Luke 1:17).

This anointing of Elijah is one that can reach the unpersuadable, disobedient and incredulous and *turn* them to the wisdom of the upright and to *love* the will of God. It's a reconciling anointing, one that *turns* the wayward to the heart of the Father and the Father to the children. Now this is a miraculous anointing!

In this hour, the Lord is sending forth His messengers, His mouthpieces, in the spirit and power of Elijah, to go *before* Him, to proclaim the "coming" of the Lord and to prepare a bride purified and beautified for the Lord.

Now instead of proclaiming:

Behold the lamb of God who has come to take away the sins of the world (John 1:29),

these ones will proclaim:

"Behold the Lion of the Tribe of Judah who has triumphed, who is avenging the cause of Zion revealing His Triumph and Victory through His prepared and Glorious Bride."

WHY ELIJAH?

I always wondered, why did John the Baptist come in the spirit and power of Elijah?

Why not the spirit and power of Ezekiel, or Isaiah, or even Jeremiah?

Why the spirit and Power of Elijah?

May I suggest to you it was because Elijah was a prophet of fire!

He restored the altar of the Lord in a time where Israel had erred from the truth and were influenced by Queen Jezebel's idolatrous sorceries and witchcrafts (1 Kings 18).

His ministry when confronting Queen Jezebel's prophets of Baal presented a picture of restoration to purity for a people of disillusioned worship. They had forgotten their God and were worshipping around a false altar. Elijah confronted this false idolatry and demonstrated to Israel through power (which just happened to manifest as fire), the true God.

We need to note here that Elijah's ministry was to *Israel*, God's own people.

And so, in many ways today, we see God's own people in the Body of Christ in this same position, deceived by the witchcrafts of man-made religion, the mixture of the world which has lured the Church to worship around a false altar. An altar of social clubs, professionalism, self-promotion and a self-serving culture. In many cases, an altar where much noise is taking place, but no signs and wonders, an altar of worship where religious rituals are being practiced, but void of the presence of God.

REBUILDING THE ALTAR ~ ALIGNING HEARTS

May I suggest to you that this paints a picture that the messengers who prepare the way of the Lord in the spirit and power of Elijah are ones sent to the Lord's *own people*. His own body, His own Church, to confront, challenge and unveil "mixture" that has crept into the worship of the saints, which like the prophets of Baal in 1 Kings 18:26-29 promote a lot of loud noise and ritual, but are void of evident power.

Those who prepare the way are ones who call a people to repentance. Repentance simply means to have a change of heart and to turn one's back on something and go in the opposite direction. The Lord through His messengers is calling His people to turn their back on mixture of the world, self-exalting worship, idolatrous witchcrafts and to turn their hearts to the one true God of heaven and earth.

The prophets of fire are coming in the spirit and power of Elijah, to bring about a true alignment and restoration in the hearts of God's people in preparation for what is to come.

Elijah's challenge to the prophets of Baal in 1 Kings 18 is a prophetic picture of repentance and alignment. It is a prophetic picture of the ministry of John the Baptist preparing the way before Jesus, demonstrating how the prophetic and apostolic ministries flow to birth a move of God.

> *Then Elijah said to all the people, Come near to me. And all the people came near him. And he repaired the [old] altar of the Lord that had been broken down [by Jezebel]. Then Elijah took twelve stones, according to the number of the tribes of the sons of Jacob, to whom the word of the Lord came, saying, Israel shall be your name. And with the stones Elijah built an altar in the name [and self-revelation] of the Lord. He made a trench about the altar*

as great as would contain two measures of seed. He put the
wood in order and cut the bull in pieces and laid it on the
wood and said, fill four jars with water and pour it on the
burnt offering and the wood. And he said, do it the second
time. And they did it the second time. And he said, Do it
the third time. And they did it the third time. The water ran
round about the altar, and he filled the trench also with
water (1 Kings 18:30-35).

The altar represents the heart, and in this case, the restoration of the altar represents aligning the heart into its true position in order for the fire to fall on it, representing an acceptable sacrifice.

We see here the picture of the 12 stones representing divine government, restoring the alignment of Kingdom Government, doing it God's way, which is not by might nor by power but by His Spirit (Zechariah 4:6).

A MOVE OF REPENTANCE IS THE PRECURSOR TO AN OUTPOURING OF REVIVAL

The sacrifice Elijah prepared on the restored alter was then saturated with water. This represents the heart of man being immersed into the river of repentance of John the Baptist, who in his own words prepared the way for one to come who was mightier than He of whom His sandals he was not worthy to tie (Matthew 3:11). One who would baptise in the Holy Spirit and fire. We know this was fulfilled in Acts 2 after Jesus' ascension where He told His disciples to go and wait for the promise. That was the infilling or baptism of the Holy Spirit which portrays the fire that consumed the altar of the Lord in 1 Kings 18:37-38:

Hear me, O Lord, hear me, that this people may know
*that You, the Lord, are God, **and have turned their hearts***
***back [to You]**. Then the fire of the Lord fell and consumed*

the burnt sacrifice and the wood and the stones and the dust, and also licked up the water that was in the trench (emphasis added).

Elijah's whole heart was to reveal to them the One *true* God, and for their hearts to *turn* back to the Lord. The way He proved this was by fire.

The prophetic spirit of Elijah that "goes before", which is the move of repentance, is symbolised by the pouring of the water over the altar. This is to prepare the way for the Malachi 4:1 fire, *"the day of the Lord which burns like an oven"*, which is the apostolic church *"released like calves from the stall"* healed, set free and subduing the enemy like ashes under their feet.

We are in the preparation process right now, where the Lord is pouring water over the altar of the heart via His messengers who carry the spirit of repentance. These prophetic mouthpieces prepare the hearts of His people, to be aligned, positioned and ready.

MESSENGERS OF FIRE

The Lord is sending His messengers to His beloved in this hour. These messengers of fire are ushering in a mighty move of repentance that will sweep the Body of Christ, like a bush fire in the Australian bush. It will blaze wild and it will cause their *first love* to burn bright!

Cloaked with the camel's hair mantle, aka the spirit of Elijah, these ones carry and release the river of repentance, calling a distracted, disillusioned, double minded, lukewarm people back to having a heart raging with the fire of love for their King.

There will be a move of repentance that will flood the people of God like a tsunami drawing them back to their first love.

Like the Galatians, who strayed from doing their deeds by the spirit, many in the beautiful Body of Christ have fallen into the trap of performance and man pleasing, bending their knee under the pressure and lure of an Anti-Christ spirit whose mandate is to mix and contaminate the altar of worship with the ways of the world. The result is a powerless people absent from the demonstration and reverence of the presence and power of God.

And as they are baptized afresh in that river of repentance the Lord will cause them to believe, hope and dream again. They will walk by faith and not sight. They will trust the Lord and no longer drink of the cisterns of the worldly mixture. No longer will they be satisfied with lukewarmness or the status quo. For this word that these messengers of fire carry, will bring a separation between those who truly seek God and those who don't. It will bring a separation between those who desire to worship in spirit and in truth and those that are happy making "noise" around the false altar.

As the Lord releases these fire brand messengers, we will see many Sunday Christians running down to the Jordan shouting, "what must I do to be truly saved?"! Some of those will be pastors and leaders who have been strangled by a system that does not promote a Christ-centred, Spirit-led agenda. For where the Spirit of the Lord is there is freedom (2 Corinthians 3:17). There will truly be a returning of many back to the right altar, and back to the presence of God. Many will forsake works for intimacy with the Lord and their own agenda for heaven's agenda. Many will find what they are crying out for, as these movers and shakers of heaven, decree and dismantle, with boldness and courage, the structures of the demonic influences in the Church.

These messengers of fire will unveil the "mixture" that has crept into the hearts of believers via the pulpits. Again, like the days of Elijah, they will fearlessly challenge the "false utterances" that have watered down the Word of God causing God's people to embrace idolatry and build a false altar of worship, all the while beckoning God's people to be a slave to performance and rituals.

These prophets of fire will deliver the Word of the Lord "razor sharp" that is going to cut to the core of unbelief in the hearts of the Lord's people, bringing about a separation between lies and truth. No longer will God's people be confused and hindered in seeing clearly because of the muddy waters of mixture. No longer will they alter between "two opinions" (1 Kings 18), and not recognise who is the One true God. No longer will they be led astray by witchcrafts and works of the flesh. NO!!!

The Lord is calling His beloved into a pure worship, worship that is in Spirit and in truth, from an altar of the heart that has been saturated in waters of repentance flowing from the Spirit instead of the soul. Flowing from the purity of the heart, not mixed with pretence or performance. For *this* is the worship which Yahweh requires as John 4:23-24 so clearly states. For the Lord in this hour is preparing His people for His coming. He is making ready the way of the Lord.

Chapter 4

A CHANGE OF LANDSCAPE

A voice of one who cries: Prepare in the wilderness the
way of the Lord [clear away the obstacles]; make straight
and smooth in the desert a highway for our God! Every
valley shall be lifted and filled up, and every mountain and
hill shall be made low; and the crooked and uneven shall
be made straight and level, and the rough places a plain.
And the glory of the Lord shall be revealed, and all flesh
shall see it together; for the mouth of the Lord has spoken
it (Isaiah 40:3-5 emphasis added).

This scripture clearly describes the process of preparation in order for the glory of the Lord to be revealed to humanity. It reveals the current landscape undergoing renovations from one extreme to the other. From valleys to plains, from mountains to plains, from crooked to straight and from rough to smooth paths. Our hearts must undergo a landscape change in readiness for His coming and the fulfilment of any decree or promise spoken from heaven over our lives.

Isaiah 40 clearly states there is a "Voice" of one crying and it comes from the direction of the wilderness. These are the prophetic instruments of the Lord, the prophets of the Lord, who themselves have been prepared in the wilderness and sent to forerun, "go before" and make ready a people for the Lord.

The voice and sound, that these ones carry, as Isaiah 40:3 explains, have the power to level out, bring low, straighten and smooth out in order for the glory of the Lord to be revealed.

PREPARATION BY WAY OF THE WILDERNESS

The seasons of wilderness between the decree and fulfilment of our promise, act as a preparation mechanism in order for us to be made ready for what the Lord has decreed and promised. We see this example was demonstrated with the children of Israel. They travelled through the wilderness on the way to entering their promised land. Isaiah 40 explains that the highway or shall we say "the way" of God is made in the desert. It is in the dry places that we are prepared for the promise that He has decreed from His mouth.

SO, WHAT DOES IT LOOK LIKE?

Isaiah 40:3-5 indicates what this landscape renovation looks like. There are 4 parts to this landscape change in the heart.

Verse 4:

Every Valley Shall Be Lifted Up

Battles are fought in the valleys. Valleys speak of times in our lives that have been unfavourable and challenging. Times of testing and trial, waging war and fighting the fight of faith. Times of unexpected hardship and struggles in life. Times where our enemies and his plans seemed exalted above us and too big for us to overcome. Or even times in our lives where we thought we won't survive and make it out of the valley alive.

According to the Strong's Concordance the word *valley* in Hebrew is *gay*, which translates: a *gorge* (from its lofty sides; hence, narrow).[1]

Various dictionaries explain a *gorge* as: a narrow valley between hills or mountains, typically with steep rocky walls and a stream running through it.

Can you picture that?

This is the same Hebrew word that David used to describe the valley of the shadow of death in the famous Psalm 23:4 KJV

> *Though I walk through the **valley** of the shadow of death I will fear no evil.*[2]

These types of valleys are not explained as flat plains between mountains, but as valleys that appear as a *gorge*. This can be likened to situations and circumstances and enemies that are pressed up against us, seemingly huge, tall and impossible to overcome. These valleys are where the fear of death and defeat surrounds us as we are found in a narrow space, even sometimes a space that seems too narrow to pass. We can experience intimidation according to the size of our situations, circumstances, troubles and enemies.

It is interesting to note the root word of the Hebrew word *gay (valley) is gevah,* which translates: exaltation, arrogance: - lifting up, pride.[3]

We see that these valleys, these gorges are times in our lives when our circumstances and enemies appeared to be exalted over us. They seem to have had victory over us and shouted, "defeat, defeat, defeat!"

But the Lord is *lifting* those valleys.

According to the Strong's Concordance, the Hebrew word for *lift* is *nasa*, which translates: to pardon, to forgive, carry away, bare, take, cast off, to bring forth.[4]

This definition speaks of redemption, deliverance, healing from our enemies.

> Surely He has **borne** our **griefs (sicknesses, weaknesses,**
> **and distresses)** and carried our sorrows and pains
> (Isaiah 53:4a emphasis added).

The word *borne* in this scripture, according to the Strong's Concordance, is the same Hebrew word used in Isaiah 40:4 to *lift* every valley.[5]

Oh, what a beautiful picture this paints! In these valley times of life's battles, we can suffer affliction, trauma and wounding.

Lifting these valleys speaks of a time of healing and restoration to those wounded and afflicted areas.

Prophets Of Comfort Who Raise And Level Every Valley

If we back up to the very first verse of Isaiah 40, the Lord starts with a declaration of comfort. It is the heart from which the Lord is motivated to prepare His beloved for His coming.

> Comfort, Comfort My people, says your God
> (Isaiah 40:1).

The Lord is sending prophets of comfort to His people to raise every valley in the preparation of the way of the Lord. These messengers of the Lord, sent to prepare the hearts of His people, carry the healing balm and presence of God. They speak comfort to the hearts of God's people, pouring out the oil of joy for mourning, granting the garment of praise instead of heaviness, binding up the wounds of the broken hearted and granting beauty for ashes. As in the true spirit of Elijah they carry the message of restoration, recompense and reconciliation. A message of hope which melts away the crippling disappointment and dejection of the valley seasons and invites the heart into an awakening to believe once again.

Every Mountain And Hill Shall Be Made Low.

Mountains represent the pride of man, the high and lofty imaginations that exalt themselves against the knowledge of God. These areas of pride and arrogance are where we rely and glory in our own strength and wisdom *apart* from His grace and wisdom. They can also be thrones of iniquity that are set against the mind of the Spirit and therefore oppose the move of God's Spirit. The Lord cannot empower or move upon a self-reliant heart, not positioned in humility. James 4:6 says that He gives more and more grace to the humble.

High and lofty attitudes of the heart are dealt with through the desert and wilderness seasons.

> *And you shall [earnestly] remember all the way in which the Lord your God led you these forty years in the wilderness, to **humble** you and to prove you, to know what was in your [mind and] heart, whether you would keep His commandments or not. And He humbled you and allowed you to hunger and fed you with manna, which you did not know nor did your fathers know, that He might make you recognise and personally know that man does not live by bread only but by every word that*
> *proceeds out of the mouth of the Lord*
> *(Deuteronomy 8:2-3 emphasis added).*

This scripture points out the reason the Lord took the Israelites through the wilderness. It was to *humble* them. The wilderness caused them to learn how to rely on God's strength and ability and not on their own natural wisdom. This process was for the purpose that they would continue to acknowledge Him when they entered into the blessing of the promised land. So, it is with us, we are taken through the wilderness seasons to cause us to realise our frailty and develop within us a dependency upon His Spirit, to be led by Him, recognise and trust His strength.

Mountains can also be pride in other people's hearts that seeks to stand in the way of what the Lord desires to do in people's lives. They are obstacles of the enemy to frustrate the Lord's purposes. But who can stop the Lord Almighty!

> *Who are you, O great mountain [of human obstacles]? Before Zerubbabel, [who with Joshua had led the return of the exiles from Babylon and was undertaking the rebuilding of the temple, before him] you shall become a plain [a mere molehill]! And he shall bring forth the finishing gable stone [of the new temple] with loud shoutings from the people, crying, Grace, Grace to it! (Zechariah 4:7)*

Prophets of Lightening Who Bring Every Mountain Low

These messengers whom Lord is sending to prepare His people are like lightning rods of God. As natural lightening finds and strikes the highest points, so these prophets will walk in the lightnings of God, they will carry the word of the Lord like fire, striking and challenging the high places of the pride of man, calling them to the low place of repentance. These messengers of fire are like fire brands in the hand of the Lord, they will challenge systems in the church that promote the agenda and pride of man over intimacy and the presence of God. They will call a people to repentance, ushering a return to the fear of the Lord and embracing the holiness of God.

As lightning in the hands of the Lord, they will break through even the hardest of hearts.

Dream: - Explosive balls of fire bringing sudden breakthrough and divine turnaround.

In my dream I saw balls of "Fire and Glory" exploding over people.

Then I saw the fire balls explode over someone that wasn't walking with Jesus and was sitting reading a book. He was seeking out knowledge and a glory bomb exploded over him, suddenly bringing revelation of the Son of God.

As I was meditating and asking God about this, I felt Him say they were bombs of breakthrough. More specifically, breakthrough in the way of *divine turnaround*. This explosive anointing was for situations of divine turnaround to the hardest of hearts. Where the presence of God's hand could and would be the only thing that could shift a situation.

A divine turnaround can be explained as: a situation heading in a certain direction with a predicted outcome which is suddenly intervened by a divine supernatural force causing an opposite outcome.

When meditating on the meaning of this dream, the Lord led me to Acts 26 where Paul addresses King Agrippa and shares his testimony of sudden divine explosive breakthrough.

In verses 9-12, Paul describes how he persecuted those who believed in Jesus as the Messiah, how he troubled, sentenced and even murdered them. But in verse 13 He reveals his encounter with the "light from heaven" that "knocked" him to his knees.

> *When on the road at midday, O king, I saw a light from*
> *heaven surpassing the brightness of the sun, flashing about*
> *me and those who were traveling with me*
> *(Acts 26:13).*

According to Strong's Concordance the word *light* in the Greek is *phos*, which translates as: light / fire.[6]

I believe it was the lightening of heaven that knocked Paul to the ground. Lightening is fire that flashes. This fire ball of glory, the lightning strike of God, interrupted Paul's direction and path of destruction and turned it around to love and life. The lightnings of God broke through a hard heart of unbelief and brought a proud murderer to his knees. It brought a man out of darkness into the light and appointed him on a journey as a minister of the Lord.

> *But arise and stand upon your feet; for I have appeared to you for this purpose, that I might appoint you to serve as [My] minister and to bear witness both to what you have seen of Me and to that in which I will appear to you, Choosing you out [selecting you for Myself] and delivering you from among this [Jewish] people and the Gentiles to whom I am sending you. To open their eyes that they may turn from darkness to light and from the power of Satan to God, so that they may thus receive forgiveness and release from their sins and a place and portion among those who are consecrated and purified by faith in Me (Acts 26: 16-18).*

One encounter with the fire of God for Paul changed the present world in His time. The gospel went to places it could have never reached otherwise.

It is the explosive fire of breakthrough that can turn a situation around in a moment and level a high and lofty mountain into a plain before Him.

As noted in the previous chapter, the spirit and power of Elijah is a turnaround anointing. As we studied in Luke 1:17, we saw that it is anointing the hardest of hearts to turn to the Father. The incredulous, the stubborn, the wilfully obstinate. It has the ability to melt the hills like wax, those things that are lifted up in pride, and cause them to turn into plains.

These messengers who carry the lightenings of God, carry a word of truth that sets those in darkness free. Those with hard hearts full of pride and arrogance like Paul, will find themselves falling to their knees meeting their Saviour.

Every Crooked Place Straight

In the Hebrew according to the Strong's Concordance the word *crooked* is *aqob*, which defines as: deceitful, fraudulent, crooked, polluted.[7]

I am reminded of Matthew 17:15-17 where Jesus addresses a "perverse" generation who had hindered faith from seeing the deliverance and healing of the man whose son had epilepsy.

> *Lord, do pity and have mercy on my son, for he has epilepsy (is moonstruck) and he suffers terribly; for frequently he falls into the fire and many times into the water. And I brought him to Your disciples, and they were not able to cure him. And Jesus answered, O you unbelieving (warped, wayward, rebellious) and thoroughly perverse generation!*

According to Strong's Concordance the word *perverse* comes from the Greek root word *strepho,* meaning: to twist and turn and reverse.[8]

This is the same implication as the word *crooked.*

Have you ever heard the saying "to pervert the course of justice"?

This means to lead astray, to deceive, make crooked, to twist and manipulate.

Various dictionary meanings of perverting the course of justice are: distortion or corruption of the original course, meaning or state of something.

This is exactly the enemy's assignment against the Church, to distort, twist and corrupt the original course and meanings of faith. He wants to pollute and water down by manipulating scriptures and even omitting scriptures from the faith.

The word *perverse* according to the Merriam – Webster dictionary is: to turn away from what is right or good, improper, incorrect, *obstinate in opposing what is right.*[9]

It wouldn't take someone with a very high IQ to look around at the generation we live in today, and conclude that we are in a *perverse* generation. That perversion has made its way into the Church.

Many have been led astray by winds of doctrines contrary to the truth, through unscrupulous men, inventing errors and using every form of trickery to mislead (Eph 4:14). These doctrines do not have to be spoken from the pulpits to influence the Lord's beloved, although some are, but the largest pulpit sprouting out evil heresies to the church in recent decades has been Hollywood. This platform of demonic social reformation has spouted out doctrines and narratives to persuade the masses to reform society to an evil agenda, and the Church has been slowly swallowing the pill. We have gone to the tree of the knowledge of good and evil and listened to Gnostics and the wisdom of this age allowing it to shape our world, our church cultures and pollute our faith. We have forsaken the tree of life, the spring of living water.

So, it is like the days of Jesus where in Mathew 17:16-17, their polluted hearts hindered their faith.

> *Keep and guard your heart with all vigilance and above all that you guard, for out of it flow the springs of life (Proverbs 4:23).*

The springs of life are meant to flow out of our heart and bring life to dead situations around us. If we have forsaken the living waters for our source and we go to another as our source, then the living waters can't flow. In the case of Matthew 17:15-17 the living waters were not flowing to heal the boy with epilepsy, because there was *contamination*.

At large the Church has given their eye and ear gates (heart) over to a message from the pit of hell. We sit and gaze upon immorality, sorceries and witchcraft and think it doesn't contaminate our hearts or our homes. We watch soap operas with a message that says adultery, fornication, homosexuality and pornography is normal and is ok. And worse than that, we allow our children to entertain themselves on such filth as well.

The Lord has called His beloved to be overcomers, the head and not the tail, above and not beneath (Deuteronomy 28). Therefore, in order to make her ready, He is coming in the spirit and power of Elijah, and he is making every crooked and perverse way straight.

His prophets of fire are sent to purify the contaminated waters where many have believed a lie against the word of God and it has taken root in their hearts. Another exciting thing about the spirit and power of Elijah, as John the Baptist explains, is that it is an axe wielding, uprooting anointing.

> *And already the axe is lying at the root of the trees; every tree therefore that does not bear good fruit is cut down and thrown into the fire (Matthew 3:10)*

This Elijah anointing goes to the roots of the contamination that causes fruitlessness. Jesus cursed the fig tree in Matthew 21:18-19 because it bore no fruit when He was hungry. The fig tree is a symbol of Israel (God's own people).[9] We are now grafted in through Jesus as spiritual Israel (Romans 11:17), and our Lord and Saviour *requires* His people to be bearing fruit in and out of season (2 Timothy 4:2). When there is a need, we should be ready to release living waters into that situation and see the Kingdom of heaven invade earth.

Therefore, in seasons of our lives where the Lord is making crooked places straight, the axe is laid to the root of things hindering us from bearing good fruit and causing us to bear bad fruit.

> *Thus says the Lord: Cursed [with great evil] is the strong man who trusts in and relies on frail man, making weak [human] flesh his arm, and whose mind and heart turn aside from the Lord. For he shall be like a shrub or a person naked and destitute in the desert; and he shall not see any good come, but shall dwell in the parched places in the wilderness, in an uninhabited salt land. Most blessed is the man who believes in, trusts in, and relies on the Lord, and whose hope and confidence the Lord is, For, he shall be like a tree planted by the waters that spreads out its roots by the river; and it shall not see and fear when heat comes; but its leaf shall be green. It shall not be anxious and full of care in the year of drought, nor shall it cease yielding fruit (Jeremiah 17:5-8)*

In order for the good fruit to flow in and out of season, we need to be planted by the living river, having our hope, confidence and trust in Him and Him alone. This is key for the power of the living waters to flow and bring life to the world around us.

At large, the Word of God has been watered down in the Body of Christ, compromise has crept in, contaminated and mixed our doctrine in order to please the masses. The direct result and fruit of this contamination has been a lack of power and demonstration of the divine authority of the Kingdom of heaven through His beloved people. This is what Jesus was addressing in Mathew 17:15-17.

Mathew 4:4 NKJV says:

> *Man shall not live by bread alone, but by every word that proceeds from the mouth of God.*

The living Word of God must be final authority in our life. It doesn't matter if we are the only one in our community believing and doing the Word, if we are to be a Noah then so be it.

When the Word of God is the final authority in our lives, we are submitted to the authority of the Kingdom Government. When we are submitted to Kingdom authority it manifests through our lives.

The living waters flow because we are drinking from the true well of life.

Prophets Of Fire Carrying Coals Of Truth Coated In Mercy ~ Plumbline Prophets!

The Lord is seeking to restore His people back to walking by faith, fuelled by the fire of their first love for Him. When His beloved is on fire for Him through restored intimacy then fruit will follow. Intimacy bears fruit.

> *"The abundance of fruit comes from intimacy with the Lord"*
> *Heidi Baker*

Truth is being restored to the ears of the Church in this hour. Messengers carrying coals of truth coated in mercy are being sent to His beloved to make straight every crooked and perverse way. There is a fire on this word, delivered with a heart of love that will purge any iniquity out of the heart.

> *By mercy, love and truth and fidelity, iniquity is purged out of the heart (Proverbs 16:6a summarized).*

Oh, the responsibility on these ones, reformers carrying insights and restoration of the forgotten truths to the Body of Christ. Oh, the weighty responsibility of the message of God, to believers who have been lost and wandering off the road of truth due to a watered-down gospel mixed with the wisdom of this world and age. Oh, the responsibility to carry the secrets of God and most important of all the *delivery* of that message.

I see more than ever in this day the Lord is raising up "plumbline prophets". Those who are called to restore truths to the Church and bring about a plumbline alignment.

A plumbline is an instrument used in building construction, to ensure the building is being built in a straight and vertical manner. Plumbline prophets are like this building instrument in the hand of the Lord over the Body of Christ.

They bring alignment so the body stays on track and doesn't become crooked in her ways.

However, I feel the Lord is wanting to remind those carrying reforming "plumbline truths", to not forget that it is by *mercy* and *truth* that iniquity is purged out of the heart of a man. Not *truth alone*.

Truth coated in mercy is delivered from a heart of humility, even though the content of the word may be very confronting and challenging. A word in mercy does not mean a fluffy, tickling of the ear prophecy which some misinformed brethren believe. But the words that need the most mercy upon delivery are the ones which are particularly confronting and challenging. These coals of truth coupled with mercy will bring about such a "turning" and "returning" of those who desire and seek to worship around the right altar.

Every Rough Place Smooth

The word *rough* in the Hebrew according to Strong's Concordance is *rekes,* which translates as a mountain ridge, a rough place and is from the root word *rakas* which means: to bind or to tie.[11]

Brown-Driver-Briggs' Hebrew and English Lexicons definition is: an impassable or mountain chain that is bound up or *impeded*.[12]

Interestingly *impeded* means: to *delay* or prevent someone or something by obstructing them, to hinder them.

Synonyms to this word impeded include obstruct, handicap, thwart, derail, put the brakes on, restrain, fetter, shackle cripple, block and frustrate.

WOW!

Can anyone relate to these definitions?

The Gesenius' Hebrew- Chaldee Lexicon explains the word *rough* to refer to: "bound up places", rugged and difficult to pass, hard places difficult to transit, calamities and adverse circumstances.[13]

Now let's take a look at the word *smooth* or as the King James version explains it as "a plain".

In the Strong's Concordance the word *smooth/plain* in the Hebrew is *biqah* which translates as: a split, a wide level valley between mountains, a plain.[14]

The Gesenius' Hebrew-Chaldee Lexicon explains the Hebrew term *biqah,* to be: a valley that is formed by a *cleaving* and separation of mountains.[15]

Cleave means to *split* or *sever.*

Biqah comes from another Hebrew root word *baqa,* when translated means: to cleave; to rend, break, rip or open, make a breach, break forth into pieces, burst, cut out, divide, tear and to win.[16]

Wow! I like how this word means to break and divide but also refers to *winning*! It is the breaker anointing to bring forth victory against our enemies and adversaries!

This same root word *baqa* is used for the word divided in Psalm 78:*13,*[17]

> He **divided** the [Red] Sea and caused them to pass through
> it, and He made the waters stand like a heap (emphasis
> added).

He broke forth against the seas, he cut and divided it and caused them to have victory!

When the Lord makes every rough place smooth this is what happens in our lives. The impassable becomes passable. He divides our enemies and breaks forth before us, breaking open a way where there is no way in order for us to have victory.

Yay! Well that is something to shout about!

The Hammer Prophets

Hammer prophets prophesy the day of breakthrough and carry a breaker anointing upon the Word of the Lord that comes out of their mouths. They wield the hammer and gavel of the Lord that brings breakthrough and justice upon the heads of the adversaries of the Lord's people.

These hammer prophets carry the Word of the Lord that breaks in pieces the most stubborn resistance. It acts as a cleaver and divides the largest of strongholds making every rough place smooth.

> Is not My word like fire [that consumes all that cannot endure
> the test]? Says the Lord, and like a **hammer** that breaks in

> *pieces the rock [of most stubborn resistance]? (Jeremiah 23:29 emphasis added)*

The word *rock* in the Hebrew according to Strong's Concordance is *sela*, which translates as a fortress, a stony stronghold.[18]

The good news is the Lord is causing those things that look like mountain ridges, impassable obstacles, adversities and calamities that try to hinder, obstruct, derail, or even thwart your mission to become a smooth plain! Where there has been delay, where you have felt shackled by circumstances sent by the enemy to frustrate and restrain you, the Lord says He is coming as the breaker to bust through all the hindrances of the enemy!

THE FORTRESS OF FRANKENSTEIN ~ SAY WHAT?

While writing this piece on the rocky fortresses and strongholds, the Lord gave me a dream which blew open revelation regarding His people and their current position in the rough places.

In my dream I heard a voice say to me which I believe was the Lord or His Angel messenger;

"The Church has been under Frankenstein because STEIN remains".

I woke up thinking, "What Lord? Whatever could this mean?"

So, a treasure hunt began. I began researching Frankenstein as I am not familiar with the story, only the familiar image of the creature that Frankenstein represents.

Frankenstein; or The Modern Prometheus is a novel written by author Mary Shelley that tells a story of Victor Frankenstein, a scientist who had a fascination with creating life and completed successful experiments which became Frankenstein's monster. This disfigured, sapient like creature endured much hardship living alone and because of his frightening appearance was rejected by everyone. This creature later seeks revenge upon his creator Victor, who began to regret interfering with nature through his scientific experiments.

Western Prometheus is regarded by some as a figure of human striving, particularly the quest for scientific knowledge, at the risk of overreaching or unintended consequences. This is also considered as one *whose efforts to improve human existence could also result in tragedy.*

I can hear you thinking, yes but what on earth does this have to do with my rocky impassable fortress?

So glad you asked! Hang in there, I am getting to it.

After briefly researching the story of Frankenstein, I realised that I am so unfamiliar with the story that I thought the creature was named Frankenstein, but in fact Frankenstein was the scientific creator himself. Which now makes sense to how I heard the sentence in my dream.

"The Church has been "under" Frankenstein because "stein" remains."

So, in essence the dream is pointing to the creator Frankenstein not the creature himself. Stay with me, we are getting there.

I then researched the meaning of the name Victor Frankenstein to see why "stein" is so significant. I separated the name.

The name *Victor* means: conqueror[19]

The name *Franken* means: son of Frank[20]

The name *Frank* means: free one, or free land owner[21]

Stein is a German word that means: stone, or rock[22]

I began to see how all the jigsaw pieces fit together.

Let's rephrase what I heard in my dream, and I will share the interpretation the Lord has shown me in regard to this research.

"The Church has been "under" Frankenstein because "stein" remains."

The Church (God's own people), has been "under" or subject to a false ideology of modern Prometheus (which roots in Greek mythology), Greek thinking apart from God. Paul called it Gnosticism. It is wisdom apart from the mind of the Holy Spirit. It is eating from the knowledge of good and evil. We have sought to strive and create and make happen in our own mere wisdom that which only is for God to do. We have stepped out apart from the Lord and have tried to be our own saviours. To no avail because "stein" remains. As in the story of Frankenstein, the scientist regrets his efforts to step into a realm of the creator that was not meant to be explored. This effort of striving resulted in his own creation turning on him.

This picture is a picture of what happens when we create Ishmaels in our lives. We try to fulfil God's promise in our lives by our own natural efforts. It then becomes our own enemy. We see this in the story of Abraham when He in his own strength tried to create the promise of God (Genesis 16). Sarai his wife was barren and bore him no children. This is a picture of our lives, our human strength is barren, and we need the Lord's sovereign empowerment to fulfil what first has come from *His* mouth. We know the story. Abraham took Sarai's handmaid and had intercourse with her causing her to become pregnant, bringing forth a son in his own strength named Ishmael. This striving to fulfil God's promise to Abraham caused great distress and trouble in his household and the strife remains to this day. The descendants of Ishmael, (the Arab nations) are at enmity against the sons of Isaac (Israel). These self-created Ishmaels cause us grief, strife, pain and come at a great cost.

They are the "stein" part of Frankenstein. Our own creations turn against us and can build stone fortresses and hindrances that are impassable and shackle us. They cause us delays, frustrations, adversaries and many a calamity.

BUT GOD!

The Lord has called us as Victor Franken, as the name means, "more than conquerors", who are "sons of the free one". We are land owners in our own right, who have been given the keys of the Kingdom to bring heaven on earth. The Lord is eliminating "stein" from this equation!

WOW!

He is sending His instruments of fire who carry the breaker word of the Lord like a hammer to smash in pieces the most stubborn resistances. Even if those stubborn resistances were caused by our own doing, the Lord is merciful in this season and is uprooting the tares from the wheat in our lives. He is uprooting all those things that have been planted by the arm of the flesh and is separating it from our lives!

He is dividing, separating, breaking and bursting forth in our lives, through all the obstacles hindering us from experiencing the glory of the Lord revealed in His appointed time of "coming".

Chapter 5

MAY I COME IN?

*Lift up your heads, Oh ye gates; and be lifted up, you age-abiding doors, that the King of Glory **may** come in. Who is the King of Glory? The Lord strong and mighty, the Lord mighty in battle. Lift up your heads, O you gates; yes, lift them up, you age-abiding doors, that the King of Glory **may** come in (Psalm 24:7-9 emphasis added).*

What could that mean "that He may come in"? It sounds like a bizarre question to ask since we are talking about the all powerful, the all mighty, King of Glory. The word "may" refers to a connotation of access being granted. Somehow His arrival depends on other factors, that something needs to be in order, or take place that would "allow", "make room" or "make way" for Him "to come in"? According to the scriptures in Psalm 24 (which we will take a look at in more detail), it proves that this is correct.

The words come in, according to the Strong's Concordance in the Hebrew is bo, which translates as: arrive, dwell, be, abide, bring forth or bring to pass, entrance.[1]

In other words, it means to show up! We want God to show up in power and in might, but the "way" needs to be prepared or aligned correctly. If the "way" isn't prepared correctly, it's like pouring new wine into old wineskins and the precious dearly desired new wine will be spilled out and wasted (Mark 2:22). As we have learnt in the last two chapters the Lord "prepares the way" before His "arrival / coming". The "way" explained here in this passage of scripture refers to the positioning of the heads of the gates.

The gates are the Church but the heads are the leadership, (we will study this in more detail in a moment). The Lord is moving by His spirit in this hour, pouring out a purifying refining fire to prepare and position the hearts of His heads (leadership) for the King of Glory to come in!

THE COMING GLORY OF THE LORD

Many in the Body of Christ have been interceding and crying out for God to pour out His Spirit afresh and to move and sweep the earth with His magnificent glory. As we know, this is what the Lord has been speaking through His prophets for some time.

This move of His Spirit is not going to pass away. It will not be a fleeting flash in the pan revival. This will be an abiding glory birthing and the raising up an overcoming generation that will usher forth the Lord's return.

How did I come to that conclusion you may ask? Well, when the Lord says He is coming as the King of Glory, know that when a king comes, he comes to reign. First, He came as the Lamb, the sacrifice.

This second time he is coming as the Lion, the King. The King of Glory! And His Kingdom will not pass away!

Psalm 24 outlines that there is a governmental positioning that needs to take place in order for Him to "come in" and rule as the strong man, as the King of Glory.

THE LORD IS CALLING FORTH A PEOPLE TO ASCEND AND STAND

If we have a look at Psalm 24 in context we have to begin with the question that is asked in verse 3,

Who shall go up to the mountain of the Lord? Or who shall stand in His Holy Place?

The mountain of the Lord refers to His presence – His habitation. We see in the Old Testament when the children of Israel were in the wilderness before they entered the promised land, the "mountain of the Lord" was where the Lord would come and meet with Moses. It was also the place where Moses received the ten commandments, the law and instruction to govern God's people. Moses was the only one who would meet with the Lord on the mountain. Moses had an intimate relationship with the Lord and had access to His presence. This portrays God's desire toward His people, redeeming intimacy.

Here in Psalm 24, the mountain of the Lord displays intimacy, glory and communion. People walking with the Lord as Moses did, now redeemed, communing face to face and abiding in the heavenly realm of glory, who, like Moses, execute the government of heaven on earth.

There are a people the Lord is calling to ascend and stand. These will ascend past the restrictions of the earth and abide in the secret place of His presence. They will abide in the heavenly governmental authority which supersedes the restrictions, limitations and corruptions of this earthly realm.

However, the question is first asked. Who shall be this people? Who shall take this position?

The answer is revealed in verse 4,

> *He who has clean hands and a pure heart and has not lifted himself up to falsehood.*

CLEAN HANDS AND A PURE HEART

This scripture speaks of purity. It describes those who have been through the refining fire, whose motives have been purified, whose works have been tested and tried.

If you feel you have been through trial after trial and test after test in this last season, it is all because He is positioning those with a heart after His Kingdom and who have said yes to the Lord in their hearts. Yes, to whatever it takes to just be with Him. Now please do not misunderstand me, I am not talking about tragedy and loss. As I noted before the enemy is the thief, killer and destroyer, the Lord is the life giver. I am talking about the dealings of the heart. The refiner's fire. The testings of our faith. The process of preparation described in chapters 2 & 3 of this book, where the Lord is levelling every valley, lowering every mountain, straightening every crooked place and smoothing every rough place. You may have felt like you have been travelling in the opposite direction of all the promises He has given you, but in fact, He has been positioning and preparing you for the outpouring of blessing He so longs to bestow upon you. The Word says that the fire is necessary, because our faith is perfected and tried and we come out as pure gold (1 Peter 1:6-7).

PURITY EQUALS A SURRENDERED HEART

Purity does not interpret as perfection. Psalm 24:4 is not saying that the Lord is desiring a perfect people, but a people with a pure heart. Purity equals a surrendered heart. Purity doesn't mean that mistakes will not be made, but it simply means the heart is positioned in a place of surrender and humility before the Lord where His will and His way can be manifested in their lives. It reflects a genuine expression of faith and is likened to Nathanael whom no guile was found in his heart (1 Peter 1:7, John 1:47).

They are a people surrendered to His purposes, who have practiced obedience at any cost and have loved not their lives even unto death. These ones are laid down lovers, having not bowed down (or as the scripture puts it, lifted themselves up) to falsehood. In other words, they are not serving a counterfeit expression of God's heart. They are not bound up in serving the systems of man and religious rituals. They are not seeking the glory of man or selfish pursuits, but are authentic in their pursuit of the King. These are the ones who shall go up to the mountain of the Lord and stand in His Holy Place.

A GENERATION OF SEEKERS

*This is the generation of those who **seek** Him, who **seek** Your face, Oh God of Jacob (Psalm 24:6 emphasis added).*

These ascenders are also seekers, because ascending is not possible without first seeking. Verse 6 reveals this generation of seekers. Ones whose priority is to seek His face. Not merely chasing the power, but to know Him intimately,

His presence being the prize, desperate to behold His face. There are no hidden agendas, nor self-promoting motives or ambitions, a generation that desires Him and Him alone.

I believe there is an awakening of that generation in this time. There is a coming forth of believers carrying His heart birthed out of a place of "seeking" and "knowing". We are this generation.

A generation I believe refers to all those of all ages living in a moment of time. It doesn't disqualify anyone of any age. So, if you are a child or in the eve of your life, you are part of that generation for the Lord. We are in that time.

To get a clearer understanding, let's look further into the meaning of certain words in Psalm 24:6 by unveiling the Hebrew meanings as per the Strong's Concordance.

Seek Him is darash which translates: To pursue, worship, inquire, require, consult, to follow.[2]

Seek His face is baqash, which translates: To strive after.[3]

Brown-Driver-Briggs' Hebrew and English Lexicon defines "seek His face" as: to seek to find, to seek the face (presence of a person), to be sought.[4]

A generation of seekers are a generation of ones who know their God by educating themselves via study, enquiry, investigation, and relentless pursuit.

This is the generation who will make way for the King of Glory.

THE REWARD FOR THE SEEKERS

He shall receive blessing from the Lord and righteousness
from the God of his salvation.
(Psalm 24:5)

This verse above explains that these seekers who are pure in heart, are the ones who will receive righteousness from the God of their salvation. They receive the blessing and what salvation has to offer, which is deliverance, healing, prosperity and salvation.

In Malachi 3:1 the Lord says he will "come" to the seekers.

*And the Lord whom you seek, will **suddenly** come to His temple (emphasis added).*

The Lord performs suddenlies in the lives of those who seek Him.

Hebrews 11:6 states that:

*He is a rewarder of those who diligently **seek** Him (NKJV emphasis added).*

However, the world operates differently than the Kingdom of heaven. The world operates and seeks to gratify self, but those of the Kingdom operate to gratify the Holy Spirit (Romans 8).

Seek first the kingdom of God and His righteousness, and
all these things will be added to you (Mathew 6:33 NKJV).

The Lord is going to come to the seekers not just the prayers. We need to seek God's heart in His ways, not just pray what we want to say. Seekers want to do things God's way, because they ultimately are seeking truth, which is righteousness – God's way of doing things and being right.

They are a generation passionately pursuing His presence more than life itself, knowing that they cannot do anything apart from Him and are in need of the Spirit of God to empower their earthen imperfect vessel (Jacob). They rely not on the religious man made systems to perform that which only can be done by His Spirit. This is the generation of Jacob that seek His face.

THE JACOB GENERATION ~ AN OVERCOMING GENERATION

Let's have a look at Jacob since his name was outlined in verse 6 of Psalm 24.

> *This is the generation [description] of those who seek Him [who inquire of and for Him and of necessity require Him], who seek Your face, [O God of]* **Jacob**. *Selah (emphasis added).*

The Lord didn't refer to him by his new name Israel, He was pointing us to a clue by describing this generation after Jacob.

Jacob speaks of a generation focused in the pursuit of their inheritance, who gain access to the Kingdom of heaven as in Jacob's ladder, and know how to release heaven on earth.

You may think Jacob was a deceiver. Yes, that is true, but if we look at Jacob's life, we find one very significant instance that changed his life forever. He wrestled and broke through into destiny. Jacob was an overcomer.

We will go on a little journey into the life of Jacob and see a clearer picture of the generation the Lord is trying to describe in Psalm 24.

Let's pick up on Jacob's journey in Genesis 32. The Lord had told Jacob to leave his uncle Laban's house and return to the place of his fathers. Jacob sends messengers and gifts to Esau his brother, whom Jacob had deceived and stolen his birthright from some twenty years earlier. As you can imagine, there would have been a level of trepidation in Jacob's heart regarding how Esau would receive him after these twenty long years.

In verse 7 of Genesis 32 it says:

> *Then Jacob was greatly afraid and distressed;*

Jacob is thinking it is D day. He is panicking. But in this panic in verse 9 he begins to return to God, the word that He spoke to him saying,

O God of my father Abraham and God of my Father Isaac, the Lord Who said to me, return to your country and to your people and I will do you good.

In verse 11 the prayer gets desperate:

> *Deliver me, I pray You, from the hand of my brother, from the hand of Esau; for I fear him, lest he come and smite [us all], the mothers with the children.*

In verse 12 he returns the promises that God bestowed upon him at Bethel all those years ago when he first fled from Esau (Genesis 28):

> *And You said, I will surely do you good and make your descendants as the sand of the sea, which cannot be numbered for multitude.*

Now we go down to verses 24-30 and see the breakthrough that took place.

> *So Jacob was left alone, and a Man [came and] wrestled with him until daybreak. When the Man saw that He had not prevailed against Jacob, He touched his hip joint; and Jacob's hip was dislocated as he wrestled with Him. Then*

He said, "Let Me go, for day is breaking." But Jacob said, "I will not let You go unless You declare a blessing on Me". So He asked him, "what is your name?" And he said, "Jacob". And He said, "Your name shall no longer be Jacob, but Israel; for you have struggled with God and with men and have prevailed." Then Jacob asked Him, "Please tell me Your name." But He said, "Why is it that you ask My name?" And He declared a blessing [of the covenant promises] on Jacob there. So Jacob named the place Peniel (the face of God), saying, "For I have seen God face to face, yet my life has not been snatched away". (AMP)

Jacob was in a position where he was done for if God didn't bless him. He knew he couldn't survive without the blessing of God on his life. He knew he needed the Lord as vital necessity as Psalm 24 says.

The force and velocity of this wrestle that comes from a place of needing God more than life itself, gives birth to destiny. It births the overcomer in your life. As we see here with Jacob, he held on and prevailed. The angel of the Lord said to him, "for you have struggled with God and with men and have prevailed". When we hold on to God more than life itself, the promises of God are birthed and we breakthrough any impossibility hindering us from coming into destiny.

Esau represents the flesh because he made covenant with the world. Before Isaac his father had even blessed him, he had married two Canaanite women (Genesis 26:34-35). Then after realizing his father wasn't pleased about this, he went to Ishmael and asked for one of his daughters (Genesis 28:8-9). Esau was trying to do things by the reasoning of the flesh. This story displays those obstacles as the flesh. Esau represents the flesh. Our flesh is at war against the destiny of the spirit breaking forth in our lives.

When we make covenants with the world it will hinder us from giving birth to our promises.

So what I see happened here is that Jacob said to himself, "If I don't wrestle to breakthrough into the promise, the flesh, Esau will prevent me from fulfilling my destiny".

He wrestled past the flesh into the spirit and from that place his identity was birthed. He was named Israel. This is why Israel as a nation has been preserved until this day. There have been many assignments against them as a people and opportunities for them to be wiped off the face of the earth as a race. But because they were born of God, they have been able to overcome any opposition that has come against them and survive. 1 John 5:4 is given great meaning in this context.

Whatever is born of God overcomes the world even our faith.

WRESTLE THROUGH INTO THE BREAKTHROUGH

What limitations in your flesh are coming after you to kill off your promise? To kill off what the Lord has promised you are? Don't let Him go! Wrestle through, and in that tenacity you will overcome whatever enemy you may be facing. You may be facing issues in your own body that are preventing you from meeting your heart's desires. Don't let go of the Lord, because the overcomer, the prevailer over natural limitations is birthed in your life in the wrestle.

This wrestle is what Hebrews 4:11 describes as "striving to enter the rest". The rest is doing it in the Lord's strength, His ability in faith. We are not striving in our own strength. In this wrestle to enter the rest we breakthrough from unbelief to belief.

Yes, Jacob deceived Esau, yes he wasn't perfect, but Esau just gave the promise away (Genesis 25:27-34). Jacob fought for it and broke through. Sometimes the Lord will have you fight for the promise and your journey may not always be perfect and pretty. Don't let your mistakes disqualify you from wrestling through for your breakthrough.

In this wrestle Jacob received the promise. He conceived the promise at Bethel (Genesis 28:11-19), but he later gave birth to the promise in the wrestle.

The nation the Lord promised Jacob would be, was birthed in the wrestle. His name was changed from Jacob to Israel in the wrestle. He birthed the government of God which the 12 tribes of Israel represent. Yes, indeed they came forth from his loins.

The Jacob generation are wrestlers who will bring forth and birth the government of God on the earth. A Kingdom Government that has the King of Glory at the helm.

We also see that redemption took place in the wrestle as he prevailed, and his name was changed from Jacob to Israel. Wrongs were made right. He was no longer remembered for his past mistakes and known as a deceiver, but he was now called by a new name, given by the Lord, Israel, which means Prince or Ruler. Israel is a nation called to rule and not be ruled. The head and not the tail. The overcomer. No longer a deceiver coming from beneath but now coming from a place of validation. Jacob had entered the rest and the blessing.

Psalm 24 calls these wrestlers seekers. Seekers wrestle until the breakthrough of promise comes. They are overcomers and ones in pursuit of God.

THIS SEEKING GENERATION CARRY AND PERMEATE A SOUND

This generation carries a sound, it's a deep groan from the depth of the Spirit resounding in the earth even now. It is like Jacob's wrestle birthing a shift and alignment of the governmental structures in the Body of Christ to make way for the King of Glory to come in. The Jacob generation is wrestling as they pursue the Lord with their whole heart. They are birthing a Kingdom Government of heaven to come on earth, the manifestation of the sons of God and the King of Glory to come in.

In March 2014 the word of the Lord came to me in a time of worship and intercession.

There is a groan deep within many throughout the body of Christ who desire and yearn to worship the Lord in Spirit and in truth. This worship not only entails a song and a melody but a walking after and a lifestyle pleasing to and led by the Spirit of God. These are a body of genuine worshippers who are tired of dead religion and the yoke of slavery it promotes.

Like the groan of the Israelites that came up before God when the children of Israel were in captivity in Egypt, likewise this groan within the people of God for liberty in the Spirit, for worship in the Spirit, for a life led by the Spirit in intimacy and reality, is being heard by the Father. As Moses said to Pharaoh, "let my people go that they may worship God in the wilderness", The Lord is coming nigh as the deliverer of his people and is setting them free from the yoke of religion and tradition that promotes and exalts man's agenda and purposes above the love of God.

This false system that portrays a form of godliness but denies the power of God is now being shaken to the very core, to the foundations, and those who hunger and thirst for righteousness shall be filled. No longer will these ones be denied access to the Spirit of freedom by the limitations of religion. For systems and structures of kingdoms not built on the sure foundation of Jesus Christ are about to be tested and proved by fire and whatever can be shaken will be shaken and whatever is of God will remain for is not the Lord an all-consuming fire?

This generation desires the real deal, the real expression of God's heart to be displayed on the earth and God is hearing their groan, the deep cry within their hearts. He is answering their cry and is bringing about a liberty of expression by shaking confinements and structures that have limited the expression of the Lord's Spirit manifesting amongst His people so that He "may" come in.

ALIGNING AND POSITIONING OF GOVERNMENT

As noted earlier in this chapter, Psalm 24 reveals a positioning of government that needs to take place to "make way" for the King of Glory to "come in". Let's continue discovering this necessary alignment and understand what must take place in order for the Kingdom to come on earth as it is in heaven.

> *Lift up your heads oh ye gates; and be lifted up, you age-abiding doors, that the King of Glory may come in. Who is the King of Glory? The Lord strong and mighty, the Lord mighty in battle. Lift up your heads, O you gates; yes, lift them up, you age-abiding doors, that the King of Glory may come in (Psalm 24:7-10).*

The definitions below are the Hebrew meanings according to the Strong's Concordance.

Lift up is naw-saw which translates: bear up, carry away, rise up, bring forth[5]

Heads is rosh which translates: head, top, summit, chief, front, highest part[6]

Gates is shaar which translates: door/gate[7]

Brown –Driver-Briggs' Hebrew and English Lexicon define gates as: entrance (space, city, town, place of meeting) a gate (of a royal castle, temple, court, tabernacle), heaven.[8]

Age-abiding doors is owlam which translates: everlasting, eternal, perpetual, ancient.[9]

Who is the doorway into eternity? John 10:7&9 says that it is Jesus!

In light of the explained meaning of these words, may I suggest how this scripture reads:

> *Rise up and bear responsibility oh you leaders, you chief, front runners. Open up the gates, by preparing a people made ready for the Lord. Create a place of opening in your meetings and gatherings, behind your pulpits and in your worship, in government and legislation. Surrender to the move of My Spirit and My ways, give Me room to manifest in your midst that I may manifest as the King of Glory and may meet, arrive, dwell and abide with My people in a tangible way! Lift up the age-abiding – eternal door who is my Son Jesus Christ (John10:9), raise Him up that He may be seen, not the name of any church, ministry or organization, but lift Him up so that He is seen. Then you will see the King of Glory come in, in such a glorious way that He will draw all men unto Him (John 12:32). Then you will see revival, then you will see the harvest of the multitudes promised in this end time harvest. Then you will see My Kingdom Come and My will be done on earth as it is in heaven.*

Those in leadership over cities, nations and churches, are to bear up responsibility and make a portal available for the King of Glory to come in. As noted, one of the meanings of gates here in Psalm 24 is temple. 1 Corinthians 6:19 says that as born again believers, we are temples of the Holy Spirit, therefore it is the leadership's responsibility to prepare the temple (being the Church) for the King of Glory to come in. Ephesians 4:12 informs us that the leadership of the Body of Christ are positioned in order to equip the saints for the work of the ministry and bring them into the maturity of faith.

Their responsibility is, to prepare a bride ready for her King. These are the heads of the gates that need to be lifted up in Psalm 24. As leaders lift up and bear the responsibility to allow the Lord's people access to His presence, the King of Glory will come in!

God is positioning His gates – His leaders, so His people have access to the presence of God. This verse resounds a call to leaders to stand up in their rightful position and turn their hearts towards Him, to rend their hearts and not their garments and to allow a portal to be opened for the people of God to meet their King of Glory.

At large the presence of God has been void in the Church. This has been because the presence of God has not been the priority of governing in the Body of Christ at large. There have been other gates and ruling systems that have been governing the Church, but now is the time they are coming down. Now is the time for a shifting of governmental structures. Now there is a changing of the guard and the Lord is bringing forth a righteous government who will rule in the fear of the Lord.

May I Come In?

Chapter 6

THE DISMANTLING OF
FALSE HEADS

Like I said in my introduction, my heart and life are driven by a passionate love for the Body of Christ, to see her come into the fullness of her identity and where needed, to break out and be set free from the clutches of the enemy's grip. As you dive into this chapter, my prayer is that you hear what God is saying and that you will understand the words that follow. Even though at times these words may be confronting and certainly challenging, they come from a place of love and deep desire to see Christ's bride rise to her glorious undefiled radiant beauty.

This chapter is longer than others, but I encourage you to engage in the fullness of the message that the Lord is trying to reveal to His beloved.

As previously discussed in the last chapter, we know the term used for government and leadership is "heads". The Lord is raising up righteous heads in this hour to make way for the King of Glory, so He may come in.

With this birthing of a new leadership or government also comes the dismantling of another.

THE SPIRIT OF ANTI-CHRIST, JEZEBEL, POLITICAL SPIRIT.

Over the years the Lord has revealed to me three main enemies that seek to hinder the "coming in" or "showing up" of the Lord by influencing and attacking leaders in the Body of Christ. They are: the spirit of Anti-Christ, the spirit of Jezebel and the Political spirit. The agenda these three principalities have in common is to weaken the Church, keep her in a place of immaturity and from knowing her true identity in Christ.

Compromise is the key ingredient and aim that all three of these demonic powers coerces the Church to surrender to, in order for their demonic agenda to be fulfilled. In this hour, the Lord is raising up a righteous government that will expose, challenge and overthrow these false heads that have set up government in the Church.

THE SPIRIT OF ANTI-CHRIST

The word Anti-Christ according to Strong's Concordance in the Greek is *Anti Christos*, which translates: An opponent of Jesus Christ the Messiah.[1]

This spirit is an opponent of the Anointed One and His anointing. Anti means to be in opposition to, and/or to be against. We know the message of hell is in opposition to the message of Christ.

Beloved, do not put faith in every spirit, but prove (test) the spirits to discover whether they proceed from God; for many false prophets have gone forth into the world. By this you may know (perceive and recognize) the Spirit of God: every spirit which acknowledges and confesses [the fact] that Jesus Christ [actually] has become man in the flesh is of God [has God for its source], and every spirit which does not acknowledge and confess that Jesus Christ has come in the flesh [but would annul, destroy, sever, disunite Him] is not of God [does not proceed from Him]. This [non confession] is the [spirit] of the antichrist, [of] which you heard that it was coming, and now it is already in the world. Little children, you are of God [you belong to Him] and have [already] defeated and overcome them [the agents of antichrist], because He who lives in you is greater (mightier) than he who is in the world. They proceed from the world and are of the world; therefore, it is out of the world [its whole economy morally considered] that they speak, and the world listens (pays attention) to them. We are [children] of God. Whoever is learning to know God [progressively to perceive, recognize, and understand God by observation and experience, and to get an ever-clearer knowledge of Him] listens to us; and he who is not of God does not listen or pay attention to us. By this we know (recognize) the Spirit of Truth and the spirit of error (1 John 4:1-6)

There are four things to note here in relation to a spirit of Anti-Christ. Let's now take a closer look at this passage of scripture:

The Spirit Of Anti-Christ Has A Message.

Verse 1:

Many false prophets have gone forth into the world.

Prophets are mouthpieces that carry a message. This scripture is revealing that false mouthpieces are going into the world and the narrative they carry is opposing to the message of Christ. It is anti which means to *oppose*. A spirit of Anti-Christ does not acknowledge and will not acknowledge Christ as the eternal door to salvation for all who accept His sacrifice. True prophesy is the Spirit of Jesus (Revelation 19:10). It will always exalt Jesus, not man or a system of man. Teaching over pulpits directing you to a system, a plan for freedom or to compromise to worldly ways is not from the spirit of truth but from the spirit of error.

Not so long ago the Lord gave me a dream that was quite confronting and terrifying. It was a warning to the Body of Christ, addressing her passivity to the message of hell that is being proclaimed in this time.

Dream – Hell's Angels

I was at a hairdresser. A client came in that I thought was either homosexual or transgender. I wasn't sure whether this person was male or female. I remember announcing to the workers in the salon, he/she had joined the "Hell's Angels". Everyone in the salon responded unmoved with a cheery response, "ok then, why don't you come and take a seat and tell us what you are wanting with your hair today". I was very surprised by their response as the term "Hell's Angels" would normally provoke fear or terror in people because they are known as an infamous outlaw motorcycle gang. I was in shock that no one had any response of fear or concern, but one worker responded rather cheerfully and said, "oh ok", as if it wasn't a big deal and it was just general information. No one thought it was concerning. The haircut this person received was interesting and different. It was a weird type of mohawk.

When I woke, I immediately understood the interpretation.

Hell's angels represent exactly what the words mean, "hell's messengers". They and their message are being groomed (hairdressing salon a place of grooming), and the Church is partaking of this grooming by being passive to its message. The message is coming from the LGBTQ movement (as in the dream I thought the person was a homosexual and wasn't sure if they were male or female) and it is a message of tolerance. The mohawk I believe represented an appearance of intimidation, to scare and intimidate anyone who would try and oppose their message.

Side note: Please do not misunderstand me, the Lord loves those ones trapped in the LGBTQ movement. In fact, the Lord has shown me that there is going to be a massive harvest of souls within that community, however the enemy is using the "movement" as a mouthpiece to influence and mold society into a twisted tolerance.

The Lord is warning His beloved not to partake in the grooming of Hell's Angels (hell's messengers) by bowing to fear and intimidation and being passive and agreeable with unrighteousness. Compromise through intimidation is helping to groom hell's messengers who carry a message of perversion and twisted tolerance, seeking to mold truths and ideals in the culture of this generation and those to come. This assignment of the Anti-Christ spirit is to pollute and defile society out of the mouths of these messengers of hell.

Rejects The Flow Of The Spirit Of God Moving.

Verse 3:

this non confession is the spirit of antichrist

This spirit will seek to shut believers' mouths from preaching the gospel of Jesus Christ, for it is the power of God unto salvation. The spirit of Anti-

Christ seeks to deny Jesus' power. It doesn't like the confession of the name of Jesus Christ.

Paul said in Romans 1:16 KJV,

> *I am not ashamed of the gospel of Christ for it is **the power of God unto salvation** to everyone who believeth; to the Jew first, and also to the Greek (emphasis added).*

The spirit of Anti-Christ will cause people to be ashamed of the fullness of the gospel. The fullness of the gospel includes the display of His Spirit and the manifestation of His presence. In some cases, leaders have watered down the Word of God that is preached behind the pulpits and hindered the display and demonstration of the Holy Spirit in the Church, because they are ashamed of the full demonstration of the gospel of Christ. They are ashamed of the manifestation of the Holy Spirit, because it might scare the visitors or offend the masses. It might interfere with the structure of their services and hinder the two-hour time slot allocated for church. God forbid the flow of the Spirit to interfere with the programs!

Ironically, and sadly, it is easier to grow a church quickly on programs, personalities and performance rather than on presence. This is because leaders in the Body of Christ have been listening and following the message and narrative of an Anti-Christ spirit, which is opposed to the flow of His Holy Spirit and seeks to gratify the deeds of the flesh.

I have literally heard with my own ears, senior leaders of very large Spirit-filled churches of over 2000 members say out of their mouths, "The flow of the Spirit is not their vision". Sorry you say WHAT? How can a church be satisfied with being void of God Himself? My mind cannot comprehend this thinking!

DREAM: A Church Under Siege

In this dream I was in my mother's house (when I dream of this it represents the Church), and I was talking to what seemed like my brother and sister in the dream. Suddenly terrorists stormed in and killed my brother and sister but I was protected. It was a very horrifying event to see my brother and sister murdered before my very eyes. I started shouting out, "it is the spirit of Anti-Christ, this is the spirit of Anti-Christ!"

When I awoke, I knew the Lord was saying my brothers and sisters in Christ are at risk and the Church is under siege by a spirit of Anti-Christ. Those who stay in the presence of God are protected from the deception of this evil spirit that seeks to murder and destroy. But those who are out of the presence are open to being taken out. The bible says that if possible the elect will be deceived (Matthew 24:24). It was a spirit of Anti-Christ that murdered Jesus two thousand years ago and it seeks to continue its mandate upon the body of Christ today.

Sadly, the doctrine of an Anti-Christ spirit has turned the Church into a social club which doesn't look any different in many ways to the world. It seeks to keep the Church out of the presence of God where they are inspired and led by the Spirit of God.

An Anti-Christ spirit will say, "Become like the world in order to win the world". Sorry but this is nothing short of mere madness! Many church movements, are steering toward this narrative in order to win the lost. *Say what*?!

Nowhere in my bible can I find a scripture reference that says, "tone down the gospel, don't let the Holy Spirit flow, be agreeable to the world's sin in order to turn them to Christ"! NO! My bible says in the day of Acts when the Holy Spirit was poured out, Peter's address to the Jews stung their hearts to the point that they said, "What must we do to be saved?"! (Acts 2:37)

Peter unashamedly answered in Acts 2:38

> *Repent and be baptised, every one of you, in the name of*
> *Jesus Christ, for the forgiveness and release of your sins;*
> *and you shall receive the **gift** of the Holy Spirit (emphasis*
> *added).*

This is what a lot of leaders in the Church today seem to have forgotten. *The Holy Spirit is a gift* given to the Church. Why would you want to shut Him down? Why would you want to hinder His manifest presence moving amongst the people? He is a gift! It is like saying to God, "No thank you, I don't want your gift. I'm happy with my carnal realm of succeeding by my own strength"! What a slap in the face to Jesus who paid the ultimate sacrifice in order that the "Shekinah Glory" could now tabernacle with men. This may sound harsh or hard, but it is the truth. When leaders shun the move of God's presence and power in their midst, they are rejecting the *gift* of God and denying God's people access to His presence. They are denying people access to intimacy.

In many Pentecostal, Spirit-filled churches in Australia, speaking in tongues in public services has become taboo, because it causes them to stand out from the world and be different or strange. They are embarrassed by the manifestation of the Holy Spirit. They don't want to look strange or weird, and justify their ideals by 1 Corinthians 14. This passage at large has been misconstrued and taken out of context.

In fact, in verse 39 Paul says,

> *So [to conclude] my brethren, earnestly desire and set*
> *your hearts on prophesying, and **do not forbid or hinder***
> ***speaking in [unknown] tongues** (emphasis added).*

The apostles of the early Church, didn't entice people into salvation through social clubs, smoke machines and flashing lights! Peter was filled with the Spirit of God to the point that people thought he was drunk, and he delivered a message that cut to the conscience of those listening. Peter, being overtaken by the Holy Spirit, didn't care about looking foolish. He may have been staggering or falling over, isn't this what drunk men do? He didn't shut down the Holy Spirit and say "Not here Lord. This will hinder the number of souls that will be added to our church today. This will offend the visitors!" NO!!! He didn't say that at all!!! Rather with boldness and power, he answered the multitude and said in Acts 2:15 (NKJV):

> *For these are not drunk, as you suppose, since it is only the third hour of the day. But this is what was spoken by the prophet Joel: 'and it shall come to pass in these last days, says God, that I will pour out My Spirit on all flesh; and your sons and daughters will prophesy, your young men shall see visions, your old men shall dream dreams.*

This Anti-Christ spirit seeks to keep the Church out of the presence of God and muse the people of God with carnality, keeping them focused on fleshy senses.

A Worldly Message That Creates Mixture In The Church, Resulting In Lukewarmness.

Verse 5:

> *They proceed from the world and are of the world; therefore, it is out of the world [its whole economy morally considered] they speak and the world listens (pays attention) to them.*

We see here that these messengers originate from the *world*. The narrative an Anti-Christ spirit will pronounce is from a corrupt morality of worldly ideals.

Anti-Christ exalts the flesh and the lusts of the flesh. It is a spirit of the world. Romans 8 says the mind of the flesh is "opposed and hostile" to the mind of the spirit. The mind of the flesh is death, decay and corruption.

So wherever you see an Anti-Christ spirit operating you are going to see a spirit of death, decay, and corruption.

It contains counsel that is rooted in sense and reason which is Gnosticism. This is an Anti-Christ doctrine, which exalts sense and reason above the Holy Spirit, the Spirit of truth.

An Anti-Christ spirit seeks to keep the Church in carnality, hence separated from her Isaiah 61 mandate.

DREAM ~ A Church In Desperate Need Of Unpolluted Spiritual Food.

This dream, I believe, highlights relevant issues the Church is now facing in her warfare with the spirit of Anti-Christ.

In the dream, I was ministering at a well-known church in a city near where I live. I was preaching on Malachi 3 about God preparing His people for Him to come suddenly. The church was divided into three sections. Section one on my left was watching cartoons on the television on the wall rather than listening to my message. The Lord showed me they represent carnal Christians wanting to be entertained at church, remaining as children (children watch cartoons). The middle section seemed more mature Christians however a man stood up with a very legalistic, religious spirit and challenged the scriptures I was teaching. In this section there were a handful who were following what I was saying and receiving the word. This section represents devout Christians who are serious in their walk with God but most of them have fallen captive to a religious/ legalistic influence. The third section to my right were looking at their watches wanting to know when the service would finish as they had social events to go to that seemed more important. This section represented the Christians who were programmed to a schedule of church and were more interested in the social event of church rather than getting fed and growing spiritually.

After I finished preaching, I didn't really feel like I had the full release of what I was carrying. I was talking to the pastor after preaching and asked him what he thought. He was slightly disengaged and I couldn't connect properly with him. I began to explain I felt I hadn't had the full release of the message I was supposed to deliver and then I stood up and shouted, "You have got to be hungry!!!! You must be hungry!!!!!" The spiritual hunger in the people was limited because they were filling themselves with carnal food. Watching cartoons, fulfilling religious rituals and social events.

Then I stood up to leave, and as I was standing at the door watching the congregation leave, they all appeared as children, who were demon possessed and walking lame. I was very disturbed, and my husband appeared (who represents Jesus in the dream) and I said to him, "Look at all these people, they are like children, sick and demon possessed! What is wrong with them?"

In a booming echoing voice, he replied, "*It's because they haven't been challenged!*" I knew it meant the Word of God was not being taught, preached or shared in an uncompromised way in order to bring about maturity, deliverance and healing in their lives. They weren't being fed true spiritual food, so their appetite was supressed for the true Word of the Lord. That is why I had to shout earlier, "You have to be hungry!" The Lord was showing me what they looked like to Him because I didn't see them like that when I was preaching to them.

God's heart is toward His people and His desire for His beloved Church, is for her to grow into maturity in love and be the overcoming warrior bride He is returning for. The Lord is dismantling structures of an Anti-Christ government that has found its way into His Church where leaders have bowed and watered down the teaching of the uncompromised Word of the Lord, not challenging His people to grow and mature, or be healed and set free. For they shall know the truth and the truth shall set them free (John 8:32).

DREAM ~ The Enemy Is In the Mixture

In this dream I was "testing" a new ride for "Sea World". I had my daughter Anastasia in the seat behind me. The ride was quite scary as we were in a log type ride and were riding in red muddy waters. I was so shocked and taken back by the "ugliness" of the colour of the waters that I said to another passenger in the log carriage, "These dirty waters are terrible!" The passenger simply replied, "Oh what do you expect, that is "Australia" for you! Red muddy waters!" I thought it looked awful and very inappropriate to have at a theme park attraction. As we continued on in the ride, it was quite bumpy and rough and very life threatening as crocodiles began to appear in the water. These crocodiles were trying to attack my daughter, Anastasia, and I was struggling to protect her. It was stressful and unenjoyable as I couldn't believe a theme park would allow a ride with such danger. I thought to myself, "I will "tell" them so!".

As I began meditating on the dream, the Lord began to show me the ride in Sea World represented the world. The sea symbolised the world and the log ride was the Church. My daughter Anastasia in the Greek means "awakening" or "resurrection", so she symbolises revival or resurrection power when she is in my dreams. The muddy waters are the mixture of the Word of God mixing with the world (Sea World). The crocodile is the spirit of Anti-Christ hidden in the muddy waters of mixture. This spirit always sets out to abort and kill off a move of God's Spirit (the crocodile was after Anastasia). Me, declaring the ride unsafe, points to my prophetic office warning the Church not to ride with the world, as the enemy is lurking to devour those in muddy waters of mixture. You can't mix the world with the Church. That is a prime habitat for the enemy to reside.

Where there is mixture in the Word of the Lord being delivered to the Church, the enemy of revival will be harboured. The latter will seek to quench a move of the Holy Spirit, because the flesh is at war with the Spirit. When the spirit of the world has been mixed with the Church, it creates confusion – (muddy waters) and the enemy so easily dwells and abides in that place ready to devour.

The god of this world rules through the carnal realm - sense and reason. The assignment of an Anti-Christ spirit is to keep a person darkened in their spiritual mind, making it impossible to understand or get spiritual revelation.

> *For the god of this world has blinded the unbeliever's minds [that they should not discern the truth], preventing them from seeing the illuminating light of the Gospel of the glory of Christ (the Messiah), who is the Image and Likeness of God (2 Corinthians 4:4).*

When a person is unable to perceive spiritual revelation they are unable to be led by the Spirit of God. Therefore, they cannot govern as sons.

> *For all who are led by the Spirit of God are the sons of God (Romans 8:14).*

Spirit of Compromise

An Anti-Christ spirit promotes a message of self-gratification and living for oneself. This is in opposition to the message of Christ where Jesus clearly stated in Mathew 16:24-25:

> *If anyone desires to be My disciple, let him deny himself [disregard, lose sight of, and forget himself and his own interests] and take up his cross and follow Me [cleave steadfastly to Me, conform wholly to My example in living and, if need be, in dying, also]. For whoever is bent on saving his [temporal] life [his comfort and security here] shall lose it [eternal life]; and whoever loses his life [his comfort and security here] for My sake shall find it [life everlasting].*

To live for Christ is to die to self.

An Anti-Christ narrative spouts: "Everything has to accommodate everyone"! What a load of hogwash! When I read my bible I don't see Jesus toning himself down to please the masses. In fact, in one sermon He had a multitude get up and walk out on Him, leaving Him with only the twelve (John 6). Those that seek to tone down their messages to appease the masses are being influenced by an Anti-Christ spirit and are not true laid down lovers and disciples of Christ.

I love what Bill Johnson, the Senior Leader of Bethel Church, Redding California, says regarding Christians who try and accommodate the world:

> *"A lot of what the Church is afraid will offend the world,*
> *actually attracts the world and only offends the religious"*

How brilliantly put! We spend so much time trying not to offend the world when all the world is craving for is authenticity and reality. The world wants something different to what they already have, otherwise why on earth would they give their lives to Christ if He had nothing else to offer? However, this is not what the religious crave. The religious crave predictability, rules and regulations.

JEZEBEL SPIRIT

A Jezebelic influenced government will rule through control (witchcraft), fear/intimidation and seduction, defiling the altars of worship into idolatry. And if not ruling through these main factors, other evidence of a Jezebelic influenced leadership is *passivity* and *toleration* to this evil.

> *But I have this against you: that you* **tolerate** *the woman Jezebel, who calls herself a prophetess [claiming to be inspired], and who is teaching and leading astray (seducing) my servants and beguiling them into practicing sexual vice*

and eating food sacrificed to idols (Revelation 2:20 emphasis added).

Often when we hear the term "Jezebel spirit" our thoughts immediately identify with Queen Jezebel mentioned in the Old Testament who makes her appearance in the books of Kings. However, the scripture mentioned above is actually a New Testament prophecy to the government of the redeemed New Testament Church of Thyatira warning "toleration" to the message of Jezebel. As a result of the Church government *tolerating* this message, saints were being swept away into sin.

Notice the scripture in Revelation 2:20 says, "She calls herself a prophetess". Again as explained earlier in the Anti-Christ section, we know that the meaning of a prophet is a mouthpiece. A prophet has a message, a doctrine to teach and proclaim. Again, like the spirit of Anti-Christ, the Jezebel spirit has a message being carried through false prophets/ false mouthpieces. This message is one that leads God's people into spiritual adultery. As we see in Revelation 2:20 the Lord correlates spiritual adultery to idolatry. What is idolatry? Idolatry is worshipping and putting another before the one true God.

Compromise is idolatry. It puts another doctrine and another message before the Word of God as absolute. It says, "Let's be agreeable to the doctrines of this age and world, to avoid persecution".

Roots Of A Jezebel Spirit Is Idolatry

To better understand the context of this message, we need to understand the roots of this demonic influence. The worship of Baal and Ashteroth were the main practices of idolatry at the time of Queen Jezebel in the land of Israel, as we see in the book of Kings. Baal was the god of rain, lightning and seasons. We see here that this worship was offering a counterfeit to the true prophetic voice of God, as it was the prophets of Yahweh who would pronounce the times and seasons of God to His people, and lightning is also a prophetic metaphor for the voice of God (Job 37:4).

Idolatries around these gods exalted the practices of sexual immorality without restraints, which invited all sorts of vile perversions, child sacrifice, sorcery, witchcraft and worshipping of mammon, just to name a few. The name Baal means husband, which is also another signpost signalling the underlying assignment of this evil as a counterfeit of the prophetic relationship God had with Israel as their husband. Many times throughout scripture, the Lord would refer Himself to Israel as her husband.

In the book of Kings, we see that it was King Ahab's (Jezebels husband) tolerance and passivity to the practice of her pagan wicked idolatry that defiled the land of Israel and led astray the nation. King Ahab knew the commandments of the Lord, but chose to ignore them anyway.

It was his responsibility as king to rule his people under the ordinances of God and protect them from pollution.

And so we see here according to the scripture in Revelation, the same is true for the government of the Church today. They have a responsibility to protect the saints from the message of immorality and mixture, sorceries and witchcrafts that this same spirit is trying to defile and seduce God's people with today.

The Consequence Of Toleration And Compromise

Now there is a reason why the Lord has an issue with those who *tolerated* Jezebel.

The Lord once said to me, *"Anita, whatever you tolerate you will be bitten by and its ultimate end is death"*.

We see here in Revelation 2:20 that there is judgement for not only those who do the practices of Jezebel but also those who *tolerate* it. This clearly displays that in God's eyes to *tolerate* is just as serious as doing the sin itself!

How are we tolerating you may ask? May I suggest it is by agreement and passivity to the message. You may not be doing the "acts" of immorality yourself, but tolerating is as good as doing it. The Lord speaks about those who tolerate her teachings and commit adultery against God *with* her. Tolerating empowers the operation of this evil. James 4 says those who are a friend of the world are enemies of God. This is a pretty heavy statement. And because the Church has been passive to the message of this world, they have positioned themselves as an enemy of God. James 4, beckons those who have positioned themselves to repent, get their soiled hands cleansed, stop being wavering between divided interests and purify their hearts of spiritual adultery. To be passive to a message of evil is as committing spiritual adultery.

We see in 1 Kings 17:1, Elijah by the authority and power of heaven declared a famine on the land of Israel because of her dark idolatry. This is a prophetic picture and warning that spiritual famine is a grave consequence the Church experiences when she indulges in compromise and toleration of evil. The lack of rain represents the lack of blessing, the absence of His presence and Spirit moving amongst His people. We see the rain wasn't released upon Israel until 1 Kings 18, after the altar of Baal was destroyed and the false prophets were slaughtered by Elijah. The mixture had to be addressed and the right alter needed to be restored.

The enemy knows the Church is useless when she is void of God's presence and power. For this reason, the whole agenda of the Jezebelic doctrine is to cause God's people to commit spiritual adultery by agreeing, being passive and tolerating this message of idolatry.

The Lord is very fervent and clear in expressing the position He requires the hearts of His people to take. The Lord requires us to be either hot or cold (Revelation 3:16).

> *Now therefore [reverently] fear the Lord and serve Him in sincerity and in truth; put away the gods which your fathers served on the other side of the [Euphrates] River and in Egypt, and serve the Lord. And if it seems evil to you to serve the Lord, choose for yourselves this day whom you will serve, whether the gods which your fathers served on the other side of the River, or the gods of the Amorites, in whose land you dwell; but as for me and my house, we will serve the Lord (Joshua 24:14-15).*

Basically my paraphrase of what Joshua was declaring on behalf of the Lord in this scripture above is, "Make your mind up, either divorce Me or marry Me but don't you play the harlot. The harlot is *self-serving*. At least have the gumption to break off your vows with Me."

We are in a moment of time where the Lord is extending to those who have tolerated Jezebel, a mercy message of repentance. It is time for the Church as it was in Joshua's day to choose this day whom they will serve! If the Church wants to move into dominion and Kingdom rulership, there cannot be mixture and the toleration of evil.

Jezebel's Agenda To Steal Identity

Not only does the toleration and practice of the doctrines of Jezebel *defile* God's people, but it also steals identity and renders them powerless by offering another view and picture of who God is.

When Jezebel was in power, Israel lost sight of who God was. Hence Elijah's address to Israel in 1 Kings 18:21 (we will visit this scripture soon). When we lose sight of who God is, we lose sight of who we truly are.

We operate from a different blueprint therefore producing fruit contrary and inferior to our true inheritance.

The Jezebel spirit's agenda is no different today, in this hour through polluted ideology it seeks and aims to steal an entire generation's identity. This then causes the Church to operate from an inferior blueprint contrary to the Word of God producing futile fruit.

The Church at large has forgotten her identity because the governmental structures have tolerated Jezebel who calls herself a prophetess. They have tolerated a doctrine and teaching that is perverse to the core and promotes a self-serving agenda.

But the prophets like Elijah are coming forth to remind Israel/the Church of who they are, her true identity. The Church are sons of Abraham according to the promise. Not idol worshippers of Phoenicia!

The Message Of Jezebel

I had a dream on the 10/10/17. This date was significant because the Lord often uses 10:10 to speak to me regarding John 10:10.

> *The enemy comes to kill steal and destroy but the Lord comes to give life and life abundantly.*

Seventeen is a number of divine spiritual alignment and also victory. I believe receiving this dream on 10/10/17 was a sign that the dream was delivering a message of exposure of the enemy in order to bring alignment and victory for the Church.

DREAM ~ The Snakes of the West

I was in what I thought was my mother's house (different from my mother's house in real life), and there was an intercession group praying in the lounge room. For some reason I knew we were in Western Australia.

As the group were interceding, a snake slithered right into the center of the intercession. The snake wanted to attack the prophets of the Lord as they were releasing the prophetic Word of the Lord. I remember looking at this snake knowing that it could strike at any moment. It didn't strike though, it was just there looking and observing. The intercessors were quite engaged in what they were praying, rebuking the snake, but the snake didn't go away, and a thought of caution and concern for the intercessors came over me as I knew it could strike at any moment. All of a sudden a multitude of snakes appeared and they were everywhere in this house and I vaguely remember thinking, "yes there are a lot of snakes in Western Australia."

Even though it was my mum's house, somehow the owner of the house arrived, and said he was going to sell the house and wanted to show it to potential buyers. I remember the front door of the house was to a bedroom. I then saw the real estate agent out the front of the house measuring the size of the house before he put it on the market.

In the next scene, there was a bedroom, which was at the front of the house. I looked on the window sill and saw a snake curled up on the front window. I freaked out a little because I hate snakes, then two more snakes appeared in the room. One was white with big bulging eyes, and the second was a king cobra. I was looking at them, worried they would bite me, but they never struck at me, they were just slithering toward me.

I remember looking up at the bed and it was half made, there was like a blanket half rolled off the bed. I remember there were Anastasia's (my daughter's) clothes on the floor, it was a bit of a mess.

Then afraid, I thought I better get out of the room because I felt like the snakes were going to attack. As I was trying to leave the room, I saw the king cobra rear up and flare its neck, opening wide, stretching its jaws and preparing to bite. I knew it was going to bite me with the intention of killing me.

I ran out of the room and met this group of people that the owner had let through to view the house. Amongst this small crowd was a young man about twenty-two years of age. I remember going out asking him for help, and even though he felt fear, he had the courage to come into the bedroom and with his bare hands removed all three snakes.

I knew he needed courage to do it. It wasn't like he wasn't afraid, but he knew it had to be done. I asked, "Did you do that with your bare hands? Where are the snakes?" He answered, "I put them way outside", I said, "*Wow you are like a JEHU!*"

I prayed many months over this dream as the full interpretation didn't come to me immediately. In fact, it wasn't until I had the dream that I shared earlier in this chapter about Hell's Angels months later, that the interpretation for this dream was fully realized. I believe these dreams are linked in their message.

Dream Interpretation:

Being in my "mother's house" represents the Church. The fact that there was intercession happening also points to the house representing the Church as Jesus said, "*My house shall be called a house of prayer*" (Matthew 21:13). Another sign that the house represented the Church was the fact that even though it was my mother's house, it had another owner. This owner is the Lord.

This house being in "Western Australia" represents the Church that is in the "western culture". The snakes (which in most dreams) represents demonic activity, assignments and presence. The fact that they first came into the prayer meeting and then infiltrated the entire house, represents the demonic influence that resides in the western culture, infiltrating the house of God.

This demonic influence of the western culture is a perverse message of compromise where the narrative of this message seeks to influence society into calling evil good and good evil. The snakes of the west (western culture) seek to destroy and contaminate the Church's (house of prayer) intimacy and birthing. We know that prayer and intercession represents intimacy and birthing. For where there is intimacy, there will be birthing.

The owner "selling" the house and showing a new group of people through, is speaking of a "changing of the guard". The new ownership through the sale of the house represents new government in the house of God. The real estate "measuring" the front of the house speaks of the leadership (front part of the house) of the house of God being measured and weighed in this season. Where the government and leadership of the Church have tolerated the snakes of the western culture and allowed its influence to infiltrate the Church, the Lord is raising up a new breed, a new occupancy that won't tolerate these snakes, removing them from the premises.

The "front" room represented the chamber of intimacy of the governmental leadership, as "front" means to lead and bedroom represents intimacy. The little cute "white" snake with googly eyes represents the Anti-Christ spirit as it seeks to hide its danger by disguising itself as "white", a friendly message of good, and secondly it was cute, so it *looked* harmless. The king cobra however was not so harmless in appearance and I knew it was out to kill me. I have engaged cobras in dreams in the past and I knew this was a Jezebel spirit. This was confirmed as I referred to the young man in the dream who later came and removed the snakes with his bare hands as being likened to JEHU! Jehu in the bible was the man who overthrew Jezebel's reign and life. So this definitely revealed the nature of this snake.

The messy bed coverings represent a house not in order and as Anastasia's name in the Greek means resurrection, her clothes on the floor represent the Church not walking in the resurrection power of God because they have forsaken intimacy. The Lord has called His Church to be more than conquerors, to be the head and not the tail, to be above and not beneath. The Church must walk in the power of the resurrection at the closing of this age.

When we leave intimacy behind, we leave behind a move of God. Revival is birthed out of intimacy. In intimacy, conception takes place and when conception takes place, birthing follows. In fact, staying in revival is staying in intimacy. Staying awake is staying in intimacy and not tolerating a contrary perversity that would seek to pollute the intimacy of the Church. We cannot cry out for a move of God and not be in the intimate chambers. We cannot expect the Lord to plonk an anointing on all of our religious rituals and worldly ideas and our fashionable plastic fantastic who ha that we do. As long as the Church tolerates the message of the western culture that does not line up with the authority of the Word of God, the Church will not walk in the awakening resurrection power of God. As long as the Church is wanting to be like the world, they won't be set apart and walk above the limitations of this world and overcome.

Myself being in the room awaking the sleeping snakes and calling for help, represents the prophets exposing and revealing the snakes (demonic influences) in the chambers of governmental leadership that have discarded revival and tolerated a Jezebel and Anti-Christ spirit.

The king cobra (Jezebel) opening its jaws wide to kill me, represents this territorial Jezebel spirit seeking to kill off the prophets and those who are pioneering a call for the Church to return to intimacy. This Jezebel spirit has sought to kill off the voice of the prophets, because these prophets are awakening God's people to see the western lie that has come into the Body of Christ causing a position of lukewarmness. The snakes' presence in the bed chambers are a picture of God's people partaking in spiritual adultery as adultery usually takes place in the bed chambers. This spiritual adultery is tolerating a western culture that carries a perverted message seeking to mold and shape a generation on lies.

The picture of myself running out of the room calling for help, represents the prophets calling forth this next generation of Jehu! The prophets are calling forth the apostolic mandate of Jehu! The true apostolic generation will put an end to the reign of Jezebel in the land of spiritual Israel, overthrowing her and seeing her influence defeated.

There is about to be a changing of the guard, a new generation is about to occupy that which is called the house of God and it will be a generation of Jehu! These snakes have been tolerated, but now a fearless courageous generation are coming in to "clean house" and put out of the room the influence of these trespassers.

No longer can the Church sit by passively and swallow a narrative of compromise!

No longer can the Church tolerate evil within its own borders, which has killed off resurrection life!

No longer can the Church seek to save its own life and reputation with the world, seeking to buy approval by watering down the gospel and sitting down where the scornful and mockers gather! (Psalm 1:1)

The Church is sitting down, but the Lord has beckoned me to tell you to arise!!!! Arise Jehu, Arise!!! Arise New Apostolic Government of the Church!

A Generation of Jehu

Jehu means "Jehovah is He", or "He himself exists". This is the real deal. This is pointing back to the all supreme existence of Yahweh. That He is He. He is the First and the Last, the One Who Was and Is and Is to Come! (Rev 22:13, Rev 1:4)

This generation of Jehu is not only going to overthrow the demonic residence that has set itself up in the Church, but like the days of Elijah where Israel faltered between two opinions and forgot who the true God was, this generation of Jehu will reveal "GOD IS HE" not only to God's people but to the world as well!

> *Elijah came near to all the people and said, "how long will you halt and limp between two opinions? If the Lord is God, follow Him! But if Baal, then follow him". And the people did not answer him a word (1 Kings 18:21).*

Elijah said, "how long will you alter between two opinions?" Mixture, confusion and double-mindedness were the fruits being born in the hearts of Israel under this sorcerous leadership.

This Jehu generation will say God is He! They will not look to man to hear the voice of God. They will not look to Hollywood as their messengers, they will not look to the universities as their messengers and teachers, they will not look to their government for salvation, but they will look to God Is He!

The one true God Yahweh! The all supreme existing One!

There is a new breed coming forth that will pick up those snakes that have been tolerated and will throw them out of the Church, out of the chamber of intimacy, while returning the Church to the house of prayer and intimacy which she is called to be. Then my friends, we will see a glorious, radiant, overcoming bride come forth, walking in the resurrection power of her King!

No longer are the prophets going to run from Jezebel like Elijah; but there is now a mantle of Elisha (the double portion) resting on the prophets, and the mantle of Jehu coming on the apostolic government. They will flow together in a higher realm than ever before and lead the children of God into a Kingdom Government.

As the Church returns to intimacy, they will return to revival and pick up those forsaken, discarded mantles and run into the world with a mandate of awakening to "Christ within the Hope of Glory". When the Church returns to intimacy they will give birth to a move of God.

It's not revival as we know it! This revival will be an awakening to Jehovah is He! The One who made them in the secret place of their mother's womb. An awakening to the Creator, an awakening to the All Eternal, the All Existent One. An awakening to the one true God!

The world will awaken to the Father's voice through His Beloved revealing the Son.

When they see Yeshua shining bright, the Salvation and Savior of the world, shining through the Church, they will come running home to the arms of the Father.

Through the movement of this Jehu generation, the Church, will be reconciled back into the image of the Son. As God is He, is revealed and restored, as *He is, so we will be*!

POLITICAL SPIRIT

In 2017 on my return to Australia from a trip to Israel, I had a very unfavorable encounter.

On my arrival back into the country, I was met with a resounding voice in the spirit and an overwhelming feeling of oppression and intense opposition. That may sound weird to some, but frequently in my prophetic walk with the Lord, He has allowed me to have these encounters in the realm of the spirit in order to reveal the enemy and expose his mandates. Sometimes it takes me longer than others to understand and clue in to what I am engaging.

I have been in and out of the country, many times on ministry trips, but upon returning I have never encountered or engaged with this principality in this way before. However, in saying that, I have engaged it while being in Australia but never fully recognized the source of the opposition I would be experiencing.

The resounding echo that was projected at me in the spirit was a "voice" that said, "You are not welcome here!" For two weeks I wrestled not fully understanding what was happening. I went from an extreme high of being in Israel and having marvelous amazing encounters with the Lord, to deep despair and travail upon my return.

"What do you mean by wrestle?", I hear you asking.

> *For we are not wrestling with flesh and blood [contending only with physical opponents], but against the despotisms, against the powers, against [the master spirits who are] the world rulers of this present darkness, against the spirit forces of wickedness in the heavenly (supernatural) sphere (Ephesians 6:12).*

Thayer's Greek – English Lexicon of the New Testament, defines "wrestle" as: *The Christian's struggle with the power of evil.*[2]

This struggle and contest is very real, as Paul clearly expresses our wrestle is not with flesh and blood, but we do engage and wrestle with the powers of darkness in the spiritual realm. This was one of those wrestles.

So I was wrestling, I was wrestling in intercession, seeking God and pursuing understanding. Then after two weeks had gone by, while sweeping the floor (yes the Lord speaks often to me while doing household chores) still wrestling in my heart, a loud resounding phrase went through my spirit that broke the wrestle. The cloud of oppression lifted, the feelings of exclusion were understood, and absolute peace flooded my heart as I heard the words of the Holy Spirit so loudly within say, *"spirit of Sectarianism"*.

The Lord then continued to reveal to me that for the previous two weeks I had in fact engaged this principality and that it stood over the nation of Australia. Consequently, upon further investigating this in scripture, I was taken on a journey of revelation and understanding of the workings, operations, mandates and fruit of this principality and its influence within the Body of Christ.

Just as a side note to my fellow Australian readers, I did have an encounter in August (2018) where the Lord revealed to me that the structures and seat of this principalities' influence over our nation were being dismantled by the hand of God and coming down. Praise God!

Let's continue,

Various dictionaries define *Sectarianism* as an excessive attachment to a particular sect or party, especially in religion and *politics*.

According to the Oxford dictionary, *politics* can be defined as the following:

1. The activities associated with the governance of a country or area, especially the debate between parties having power.

2. The principles relating to or inherent in a sphere or activity, especially when concerned with power and status. *Synonyms: power struggle, manipulation, opportunism.*

3. Activities aimed at improving someone's status or increasing power within an organization.[3]

We see here politics defined, refers to the debate between parties, and fundamentally the debate is rooted in the need for power and recognition. Hence the correlation of sectarianism and the operation of a political spirit.

Paul warns the Church of this "party spirit" many times in his epistles.

> *Now the doings (practices) of the flesh are clear (obvious):*
> *they are immorality, impurity, indecency, Idolatry, sorcery,*
> *enmity, strife, jealousy, anger (ill temper), selfishness, divisions*
> *(dissensions), party spirit (factions, sects with peculiar*
> *opinions and heresies) (Galatians 5:19-20 emphasis added).*

We see here that the party spirit/political spirit is a practice and work of the flesh. In Galatians 5:20 it is noted as a *spirit*, thus it has power to influence a heart not fully surrendered to the Lord's ways, operating by the flesh and seeking to gratify the flesh. How you may ask? Let's take a look at the out workings, mandates and fruit of this spirit.

Orphan Mindset

The greatest doorway for this spirit to hook into the governmental structure of the Church is through people with orphan mindsets. A political spirit at its roots, seeks to *identify* with someone or something (organization, denomination etc.) rather than being rooted and grounded in their identity in Christ.

> *But I urge and entreat you, brethren, by the name of our*
> *Lord Jesus Christ, that all of you be in perfect harmony*
> *and full agreement in what you say, and that there be no*
> *dissensions or factions or divisions among you, but that*
> *you be perfectly united in your common understanding and*
> *in your opinions and judgements. For it has been made*
> *clear to me, my brethren, by those of Chloe's household,*
> *that there are contentions and wrangling and factions*
> *among you. What I mean is this, that each one of you*
> *[either says, I belong to Paul, or I belong to Apollos, or I*
> *belong to Cephas (Peter), or I belong to Christ. Is Christ*
> *(the Messiah) divided into parts? Was Paul crucified on*

behalf of you? Or were you baptized into the name of Paul?
(1 Corinthians 1:10-13)

Here we see the Corinthians being very mislead as they were trying to identify with a natural leader rather than Christ. Paul was saying if you are identifying with a person, *other* than Christ it leads to division, dissensions and strife.

EVEN
BETHEL IRIS, ETC.

The natural man wants to *identify* with someone or something prominent or successful. This behavior quenches authenticity as it produces clones of people wanting to be like what they identify with. That is why we may hear Christians say, "Oh I'm from this movement/church, or I'm from that movement/church." They identify with the organization rather than the Lord. Paul says doing such things creates divisions, factions and sects. In fact, by saying that, it comes from a place of pride expressing the notion of superiority and inferiority. I'm better or our church is better, or my pastor is better. This creates divisions, contentions and wranglings as Paul pointed out. When people identify with what they think is successful or prominent (meaning fame or notoriety), rather than Christ alone, they are placing their identity in a carnal ideal and not walking out their relationship with Christ intimately. Christians who engage in such behavior will remain shallow in their growth and maturity.

I have literally been in conversations where people have tried to evangelize me to go to their church. Friends, we are not to be evangelizing other Christians out of their churches because we think our church is the "be all and the end all". This is pure arrogance and pride, and it is a mindset of the flesh, displaying carnal Christianity, which in actual fact is immaturity.

We have been commissioned to go ye into all the world and evangelize the lost, not evangelize and fish out of other people's ponds or watering holes (Mark 16:15-16). Stealing sheep from other pastures, is a political spirit at work. Paul said this behaviour is just not on!

We need to honor and respect the wonderful differences in the body, the different roles, functions and unique identities, prominent or hidden, famous or not, large or small. Then we will see the harmony and unity Paul so deeply yearned to see the Lord's body functioning in.

> *For you are still [unspiritual, having the nature] of the flesh [under the control of ordinary impulses]. For as long as there are envying and jealousy and wrangling and factions among you, are you not unspiritual and of the flesh, behaving yourselves after a human standard and like mere (unchanged) men? For when one says, I belong to Paul, and another, I belong to Apollos, are you not proving yourselves ordinary unchanged men? What then is Apollos? What is Paul? Ministering servants [not heads of parties] through whom you believed, even as the Lord appointed to each his task: I planted, Apollos watered, but God [all the while] was making it grow and He gave the increase. So neither he who plants is anything nor he who waters, but only God who makes it grow and become greater. He who plants and he who waters are equal (one in aim, of the same importance and esteem), Yet each shall receive his own reward (wages), according to his own labor (1 Corinthians 3:3-8).*

Paul here is strongly identifying in this passage that each joint supplies. No one is greater or more important in their work but each function is *equal* in its necessity. He states only God as the greater One bringing about the outcome of that which has been sown.

Carnality will seek to bring attention to man. However, the fruit of spiritual maturity will be to focus attention on the Lord. Basically Paul is saying here, with these mindsets and ways of thinking, you are still babies. As long as the flesh is ruling, division will be among you.

Political Spirit Is Essentially About Power

As noted above, the definition of politics has an overwhelming theme, referring to the need for power and the wrestle that goes on to maintain or gain power. A politically influenced government produces self-serving leaders who won't lay down their lives for those they lead because they are sadly in it for themselves. Someone motivated or under the influence of a political spirit will do anything to save his/her reputation in order to *maintain* or *gain* power. Those under this influence will willingly engage and *play the game* of politics in order to gain, keep or maintain position and recognition.

Playing The Game

A church government under the influence of a political spirit will fail to be authentic in nature as the systems behind this spirit's operation require "playing the game". The "game" of gaining favor, recognition, promotion and influence have a set of rules to play by. These rules can even be ethical and "Christian" in nature. They are not always evil or carnal necessarily, but they are motivated by a carnal agenda and to uphold these rules, you will have to compromise and sell out to stay in the game. If you cross those game set rules, you are most commonly excommunicated out of favor with the sects and clicks.

A politically driven organization creates a bunch of rules to follow with methods and systems to uphold at all costs. It partners with a religious spirit. Religion upholds law rather than relationship. When that joins forces with a political spirit, it is very good at maintaining division. A political spirit will encourage the use of politics over truth in governing. The Pharisees in Jesus' time were a typical example of this. They fiercely wanted to uphold their laws, traditions, and policies over receiving the truth of the gospel Jesus came to earth to give.

The grave problem the Church has faced in advancement has been the fact that at large the governmental structure and culture of the Body of Christ have been a slave to this spirit.

We know in secular government, politicians are well known to take on the identity of a chameleon in order to keep the favor with the people, even if it means compromising the truth. So those that serve this political spirit, focus on/prioritize upholding their reputation, power and influence at all costs. Hence great compromise has entered the Church and we have bowed to a spirit of politics that has endorsed "political correct behavior".

Political Correctness, The Trap Of The Church, That If Unmarked Will Essentially Be Her Grave

The term "politically correct" refers to language, policies, or measures that are intended to *avoid offense.*

There has been a very unhealthy sweep of politically correct indoctrination seep into the Church culture at large that seeks to prioritize retaining reputation and favor over the truth of the gospel. We have watered down terms we use when presenting the gospel in order not to offend anyone.

I love what prophetic writer and blogger Dawn Hill says in her article on a Church without apology:

> *"If our personal version of the gospel is edited for content so that it is suitable for the carnal nature of a person, then it is not authentic but rather apologetic. I am increasingly aware of the heart of the Father drawing us back to what truly matters, and every facet of Him matters. Stop apologizing, church. The authentic gospel and Presence of the Holy Spirit offends, brings persecution and multiplies the church.*

Areas where the Body of Christ has been spiritually ill will be healed by authenticity only found in Him. We are on the precipice of something of astronomical proportions. It does not come with bowing to the culture in the world. It comes when the church takes her place and without apology establishes the counterculture originating from the throne room. This is a church without apology".[4]

She further explains that the Body of Christ is in desperate need of a reformation. This reformation does not apologize for a gospel that is mindful of someone else's eternity! Well said Dawn!

Sadly, somewhere along the way the Church has gone out of her way to avoid any sort of persecution at all costs. This is absolute evidence of a politically influenced governmental body. We have been discouraged to say *"strong"* words like repent, sin, or idolatry. These words have become taboo over most pulpits in the western world. Why? It's not politically correct. This language might *offend* people. Instead the thinking is, "Let's repackage those words by watering them down and not call the elephant in the room, in order not to offend people". Well Jesus had some news for that type of thinking. Motivated by intense love, Jesus on many occasions ran the risk of offending people by delivering the truth to them. One instance that comes to mind was in John 6:55-56.

For My flesh is true and genuine food, and My blood is true and genuine drink. He who feeds on My flesh and drinks My blood dwells continually in Me, and I [in like manner dwell continually] in him.

In verse 60 it is evident that His own disciples struggled greatly with this message.

When His disciples heard this, many of them said, this is a hard and difficult and strange saying (an offensive and unbearable message). Who can stand to hear it? [Who can be expected to listen to such teaching?]

Jesus' words of truth, offended them. It was hard for them to hear. It was *offensive* and even *strange!* Jesus responded to them in verse 61.

Is this a stumbling block and an offense to you? [Does this displease and shock and scandalize you?] What then will your reaction be if you should see the Son of Man ascending to [the place] where He was before?

So it is today in society, truth has become hard to hear. In this translation in the amplified classic version, Jesus' sayings were explained as *scandalizing* and *shocking.* So it is in our western society. Truth has become shocking to hear because it has been so watered down and compromised. Truth almost sounds like heresy to those influenced by an Anti-Christ influenced culture and a politically driven society. Truth is strange, foreign even, to the ears of those who partner with the realm of sense and reason.

Why is truth so important? Jesus was quoted saying in John 8:32,

And you will know the Truth and the Truth will set you free.

The truth is important because it delivers freedom. When we uphold a system that promotes compromise to the truth, we are then endorsers of bondage!

Territorial

A political spirit is anti-unity and is territorial in nature. Something that is territorial relates to *ownership.* People can be territorial in churches when it comes to positions and departments. This attitude is anti-unity and desperately seeks to maintain authority over a region, position, place, church, organization etc. It defends its boundaries and aims to keep out anyone who may threaten their power and rule. As mentioned before, those operating under a political spirit are driven by the need for power and recognition, so anyone who could possibly dismantle or challenge this agenda is seen as a threat.

The Son of God encountered this horrific spirit when He walked the earth. The Pharisees were driven by a political spirit, founded on the pride in their hearts and their need to maintain power and recognition from people (Matthew 23). Jesus and the message He carried, were an absolute threat to this paradigm, hence their desire to kill him.

However, we see this political spirit manifested earlier in Jesus' life in Matthew 2 when Herod had a visitation by men from the east. Upon learning about the birth of a king and realizing his position could be threatened and the power of his kingdom challenged, he ordered the death sentence of all baby boys two years and under. This spirit is ruthless in its quest to maintain power. Murder, persecution and bullying are evident fruits of a political spirit in operation.

Jesus' mandate was freedom to the captives and this political spirit vehemently opposed Him, keeping Him out of the very territory He was called to effectuate the greatest impact on, His own people.

A political spirit's identity is rooted in territory not freedom. As previously discussed, a political spirit operates from an orphan mindset and the roots of an orphan mindset are abandonment or rejection. So the operations of this spirit is rejection. It rejects in order to maintain territory.

It seeks to "keep you out" of your jurisdiction. It says, "you are not liked, welcome, or wanted here." It uses the very thing at its roots as a weapon. REJECTION.

Competitive

A territorial mentality is competitive at its core. It masks a false sense of unity. But it is very selective of who can join that movement. That's why I'm not a fan of movements. I didn't say they were evil, I'm just not a fan of them. Because movements can become *exclusive.* Where there is exclusive thinking, there is an anti-unity mentality. It promotes a territorial way of thinking and rejects the unique individual needs and functions of various parts of the body (1 Corinthians 12:12-27).

We need to remember there are different streams and expressions in the Body of Christ. Jacob spoke different blessings over His sons, unique to them and their heritage. These then became the tribes of Israel, all functioning from a distinctive, individual expression (Genesis 49). So it is with the Body of Christ, there are different parts and members in the body functioning accordingly. But if identity becomes exclusive, "we are better than you" type of thinking, it is sectarianism and a political spirit.

Again, a competitive mindset comes from an orphan foundation of fulfilling the need to "prove" ourselves. It is rooted in selfish ambition and its identity is fashioned and founded upon who we can "out do", or who we are "better" than. A "competitive" spirit denies true unity in the Body of Christ. True unity is forged through true humility. True humility is a product of knowing your true identity. When you truly know who you are in Him, you know you are nothing without Him. When we do what the Father inspires, leads and empowers us to do, we have no need to compete or "out do" someone else.

Hence why Paul addressed the Corinthians and called out this carnal behaviour of comparing themselves to one another. "I'm from Paul, I'm from Apollos", is a carnal way of thinking. Competition is carnality! The Church is of no use to anyone when they are rooted in carnality.

The Antidote: Humility The Foundation Of Unity

One day while praying for unity amongst the Christian leaders and churches in my city, I was asking the Lord for keys and strategies. Then I heard a phrase resound in my spirit,

Unity will manifest where sonship is demonstrated!

I immediately understood what message He was conveying to me. When the Body of Christ is rooted and grounded in their identity in Christ, they mature as sons. They find no need to compete with one another because they know who they are in their individual function and expression, and celebrate the unique differences of their brothers and sisters. Their identity is rooted in Christ and no longer in their own carnal striving. As a result, perfect love has matured in their lives to the point that they no longer operate from a place of fear driving them to "prove" themselves and "out do" their fellow brethren.

However, as we have just read, a political/party spirit *promotes* competition. It sprouts, "I'm better!", "No, I'm better!" Paul said that's all hogwash! A mindset that seeks superiority, always striving to be "better" than their fellow brethren is an orphan mindset which is detached from the heart of Christ.

As I noted earlier, the spirit of unity will be found or evident where there is a Spirit and heart of humility. Pride on the other hand, breeds contention and strife. The outcome of contention is division.

*Only by **pride** cometh contention: but with the well advised is wisdom (Proverbs 13:10 KJV emphasis added)*

Pride is self-focused, and fights for its own cause. It is self-seeking at its core and resists being vulnerable or yielded. It will defend its own agenda rather than yield to reason. To be team players we must submit one to another.

*Likewise, you who are younger and of lesser rank, be subject to the elders (the ministers and spiritual guides of the church)-[giving them due respect and yielding to their counsel]. Clothe (apron) yourselves, **all** of you, with humility [as the garb of a servant, so that its covering cannot possibly be stripped from you, **with freedom from pride and arrogance**] toward one another. For God sets Himself against the proud (the insolent, the overbearing, the disdainful, the presumptuous, the boastful)-[and He opposes, frustrates, and defeats them], but gives grace (favor, blessing) to the humble (1 Peter 5:5 emphasis added)*

There is no presence of God, where pride has created division, as we see clearly in this verse. God resists the proud. This means His grace (empowerment, power, favor, blessing and *presence)* is absent. We see a great absence of the latter in the Body of Christ at large. Could a key be the presence of a political spirit influencing the culture of our governmental leaders in order to keep the Church ineffective, immature, carnal and out of the presence of God?

Psalm 133:1-3 reveals why God commands a blessing where the people dwell in unity.

Behold, how good and how pleasant it is for brethren to dwell together in unity! It is like the precious ointment poured on the head, that ran down on the beard, even the beard of Aaron [the first high priest], that came down upon the collar and skirts of his garments [consecrating the whole body]. It is like the dew of [lofty] Mount Hermon and the dew that comes on the hills of Zion; for there the Lord has commanded the blessing, even life forevermore [upon the high and the lowly].

The oil mentioned in this verse is the anointing. The anointing, the presence, will be present where there is unity amongst the brethren. Where agendas have been laid down for the greater cause of Christ and where the brethren have clothed themselves with humility, serving one another.

The Lord has called us to be team players. The foundational thinking of a team player is to grasp that we need each other to accomplish our goal.

An independent spirit exudes an attitude of superiority and arrogance and doesn't recognize the need for others reaching the goal. You can't submit to someone you don't honor. Honor means to hold someone in high regard and respect. So if there is no regard or respect for each other, this then defuses the ability to submit to one another.

Thus, relating that to a corporate picture of harmony in the Body of Christ, if we all commit to our own function and don't try to be someone else, the power in this unity will massively annihilate the enemy's capacity and keep God's purposes unhindered.

> *Therefore, humble yourselves [demote, lower yourselves in your own estimation] under the mighty hand of God, that in due time He may exalt you, Casting the whole of your care [all your anxieties, all your worries, all your concerns, once and for all] on Him, for He cares for you affectionately and cares about you watchfully*
> *(1 Peter 5:6-7).*

The antidote to the influence of a political spirit operating and fulfilling its agenda of division amongst the brethren, is truly surrendering to the hand of God and trusting that He will take you where you need to be when you need to be there. All striving, the need to self-promote and frustration will leave, and the peace of God will rule in your heart, guarding against anxieties and cares you may be experiencing.

In the waiting process we suffer anxieties and cares. Therefore, the Lord beckons us to cast those cares on Him, for He cares for us. He cares that we have concerns about the parts in the process we don't understand. He cares that we may struggle in faith and trust. He cares about the things we wrestle with in our hearts. He cares! Cast the care and let Him exalt, promote and get you to where you need to be on His time schedule and trust that He has your best interests at heart in the process.

Chapter 7

CHANGING OF THE GUARD ~A NEW WINESKIN OF DIVINE GOVERNMENT

While writing this book, there was a season when the Lord kept bringing before me the numbers 12:12. I would see this on my phone, microwave, computer and car clock. It seemed everywhere I looked in this particular season, all I would see were the numbers 12:12. When asking the Lord about this, He reminded me that 12 signified "divine government" or "The Government of God". The Lord revealed to me that He is aligning His people to His divine government on the earth in this season.

A DIVINE GOVERNMENT OF AUTHORITY AND POWER

Government is an authority word. Any type of government possesses authority and power to create rules and to enforce them. His Kingdom is emerging and with a righteous government carrying the authority and weight of heaven. In other words, the King of Glory is coming in and empowering His Church as a divine government to flow and demonstrate heaven's authority and power on the earth.

WE RULE FROM THE HIDDEN PLACE

One day during my precious prayer time with the Lord, I was caught up in an encounter where I began to see and experience a sovereign move of His Spirit upon His Church about to take place in the coming months and years. This encounter is difficult to describe in words, because you would have to experience it to understand it. I saw the Lord coming and meeting with His people in the fullness of His person, but I was overwhelmed with the power and authority of His manifest presence. I immediately saw the necessity of being "hidden" in Him because those not "hidden" in Him would not be able to contain or flow with the velocity of power of His "meeting".

> *For [as far as this world is concerned] you have died, and your [new real] life is **hidden** with Christ in God. When Christ, who is our life, appears, then you also will appear with Him in [the splendour of His] Glory (Colossians 3:3-4 emphasis added).*

Isaiah 9:6 says the government of God has been put upon Messiah's shoulders. This means only HE can carry heaven's power and authority. Only His shoulders can carry that, because He paid the ultimate price. Colossians 3:3 says, through salvation we are *dead* to this world and now are "hidden *in* Christ". Therefore, we can carry heaven's authority *through* Christ, by being *hidden* in Him. We cannot carry heaven's authority and power *separate* from Christ, nor operate in it in our own strength, human wisdom, efforts or means. We cannot create separate from the Holy Spirit's leading and expect heaven's endorsement of power and authority to be upon it. Anything created or done outside the Holy Spirit's leading is not birthed of God. It is carnal. It may be a "good" thing, but not a "God" thing. Good things don't overcome the world. Only God things do.

"Good" things usually hold an earthly agenda for the glorification of man. "God" things always maintain a heavenly agenda for the glorification of God and for the better purpose of man.

> *For whatever is born of God is victorious over the world, and this is the victory that conquers the world, even our faith (1 John 5:4).*

It is those things born of the Spirit of God that will endure the attacks in the world. Because they are birthed from the Spirit, they are *not* subject to death, decay and corruption. Likewise, only things birthed from the Spirit of God will be able to carry and maintain the *weight* of His Glory.

Now continuing on in the second part of verse 4 of Colossians 3, to *appear* with Him in the splendour of His glory is impossible for those who have not died to the lusts and dictates of the flesh. When there is still a desire to be "seen", death has not taken place. But those hidden in Christ, who have no earthly desire, are able to appear with Him in the splendour of His glory. Meaning that they will demonstrate heaven's authority and power in the time of His appearance, as a sovereign move of God. A sovereign move is when "He appears" or "comes in". Those truly hidden, are those who yearn for Christ alone to be seen and reach out to humanity, displaying His wonders on earth.

This heart position is the platform of purity that the government of heaven flows from. True authority of heaven is released through believers who are hidden in Christ. They have no need or ambition to be seen, they desire no fame or notoriety. They only find their identity in Him. These ones demonstrate true kingdom authority and power, subduing nations, and walking in the fullness and original purpose given to man in the garden of Eden. Executing dominion over all the earth! (Genesis 1:28)

CHANGING OF THE GUARD

As revealed in Psalm 24, the "heads", who are the leaders of the Body of Christ, carry the responsibility of allowing the King of Glory to "come in" and abide with His people.

When pondering on this word and searching out the heart of God in relation to His strategy, the Word of the Lord came to me saying;

> *"There is coming a shift of government in the Body of Christ in this hour, from the House of Saul to the House of David, from the House of Vashti to the House of Esther."*

As I meditated on this word, I had a light bulb moment. These two scenarios in the scriptures so perfectly paint a picture of a transfer of governmental leadership that took place for the "sake" of *His* kingdom.

NEW WINESKIN GOVERNMENT

There is a new wineskin of leadership that the Lord is bringing forth in this hour, ones who are after God's heart like David and love not their lives even unto death like Esther. True courageous, sold out leaders with pure hearts who will lead God's people into victory. Surely these leaders will confront the Goliaths and expose the Haman's. As the Lord says in Psalm 37:13 AMP version:

He laughs at the wicked for He sees that their own day [of defeat] is coming.

The enemy's "day" is up and it is time for God's people to arise in victory, might and strength as they are being led, trained and equipped by this new wineskin leadership.

In January 2017 the Lord spoke to me saying,

"In these days and the days to come, I am raising up "wrecking ball reformers" in the Body of Christ, with the forehead of John the Baptist, who will challenge the hidden hypocrisies and religious systems that bear no Kingdom fruit, keeping My people enslaved to religion and tradition."

There is a reformation of truth taking place in the Church right now, which is going to give birth to a REVOLUTION. This revolution is not one of violence and hatred, but of raging *love* and *passion,* turning darkness on its head and bringing liberty to the captives.

These rising "wrecking ball reformers" are not going to wreck lives or hearts but will wreck demonic lies and systems that betray God's people into living a life less than what His blood was shed for at Calvary.

Reformers challenge systems of man-made ideals, reveal truth in the scriptures and expose hypocrisies in self-serving agendas. God is raising up a new government in the Church "for the people". This is the David and Esther Government.

THE SHIFT OF GOVERNMENT ~ THE RISING DAVIDS AND ESTHERS

Saul and Vashti represent a self-serving government, but God is raising up leaders in this hour with the heart of David and Esther, who minister first unto the Lord and then serve the people. Those like Esther put their lives on the line for the sake of saving God's people. These selfless leaders are true shepherds who will lay down their lives for His cause and fear Him before people. And just as David restored the ark (the presence of God to the people) and danced stripped bare before God and man, so are the Davids arising in this time stripped of performance, rituals, dignity, honor, titles, self-serving agendas, selfish ambition and reputation. They are completely abandoned to the cause, love and pursuit of the King.

Their mandate of heaven is to restore the presence of God back to the people and pull down the religious and worldly structures denying God's people access to His presence.

This new leadership know their God, and do mighty exploits. They are trained and equipped, worshippers in intimacy, coming from the wilderness like David and slaying the giants that have taunted God's people for generations.

This new leadership is going to give birth to the overcomers!

They will lead with courage and faith. They will lead with love and grace. They will lead with compassion and might.

They will lead with the FEAR OF THE LORD!

THE SEASON OF TWEAKING AND REFINING, SIFTING AND SHAKING

In this season, God is tweaking and refining His new emerging government. Although David and Esther were appointed and anointed by God for divine assignments on earth, they still bore obstacles in their flesh that needed aligning, in order to bring forth the mandate of heaven on earth. God is now pouring His refining fire upon His vessels as the final alignment for the glorious outcome.

Esther's Refining and Glorious Outcome

As Esther was called for such a time as this to petition the king on behalf of her people, she had to overcome fear that was trying to hinder her from fulfilling her mission (Esther 4). But thanks to the firm counsel from her cousin Mordecai who challenged her fear and reminded her of her calling, she died to her fear and proclaimed, "*if I perish I perish*" (Esther 4:16). These historic words will be the mantra of a rising leadership, who have died to their own agenda, their own ways and have yielded to heaven's mission. They will walk in resurrection power and see the impossible made possible in the name of their King. They will walk in the light of the glory of the King which relates to the meaning of Esther: star/bright light. This is symbolic of a government rising in the righteousness of the King shining as the noonday sun (Psalm 37:6).

David's Refining Before the Birthing of a New Era

Many leaders who are called to be Davids in this season, are going through a final refining and aligning in order to give birth to the Kingdom mandate that God has put inside of them. A perfect example is when David had in his heart to bring back the Ark of the Covenant as a centerpiece of worship before Israel. The Ark had been stored in the house of Abinadab for the entire duration of the judging of Samuel and the reign of king Saul in Israel.

David addressed the assembly of Israel putting forth this desire and mandate burning in his heart.

> *And David said to all the assembly of Israel, If it seems good to you and if it is of the Lord our God, let us send abroad everywhere to our brethren who are left in the land of Israel, and with them to the priests and Levites in their cities that have suburbs and pasturelands, that they may gather together with us. And let us bring again the ark of our God to us, for we did not seek it during the days of Saul (1 Chronicles 13:2-3).*

This same mandate is upon this new emerging government, to restore the presence of God as the centerpiece and focal point of His people. Notice, they did not seek it during the days of Saul. This clearly reveals that a Saul government is not interested in the presence of God.

Hence, why there is a shift of government from the House of Saul to the House of David. The presence is being restored to His people.

However, in the process of fulfilling this mandate, David found himself trying to do this with the arm of the flesh. Even though the goal was noble and pleasing to God, the *way* he first went about it wasn't. In fact, the scriptures say that God's anger was kindled against them. (2 Samuel 6:7)

For those of you who aren't familiar with the story, David's first attempt at bringing the Ark into Jerusalem, was done out of order to God's command. There was a *way* God had ordained for His Ark to be handled, but David did not show the reverence or respect for God's command and decided to do things his way (1 Chronicles 13:7-14).

According to 1 Chronicles 15:15, the Ark of the Covenant was to be carried upon the Levites' shoulders, but David thought well, "I've got this, I've got this vision from God, I'm going to make a "new wagon" and put the ark on that!" Can you see where I am going with this? Yes, we try to accomplish

God's given vision with all these new ideas, programs, events, church systems, structures i.e. the "new wagon", do it in the arm of the flesh through performance and try to hitch God's presence on it!

The Lord is saying, "*I will not ride on a "new wagon" made with the hands of man*"!

In this first attempt of bringing the Ark into Jerusalem, David had a great procession of singing, praising and sacrificing going on. Oh, the show must have been amazing! But it didn't impress God one bit. Sometimes what impresses man (the show, the lights, the fan-fare and the who ha), doesn't impress God.

He simply requires things to be done *His way*, not all our grand ideas and new designs.

We then see the oxen that were pulling this beautiful looking cart the Ark was placed upon, stumble at the threshing floor. As Uzzah put his hand out to steady the Ark, God's anger was kindled against him, He smote him, and he died (2 Samuel 6:6-7). Consequently, David became angry and offended at God for not endorsing his lack of reverence for His presence!

Sometimes we can get offended at God for not honoring our works and efforts to achieve *His will* outside of His ways!!!

God's will must be done God's way! Yes, it's His way or the highway!

Those acquainted with God's presence can become familiar with it, losing reverence and respect for that which is *holy*. Even though David was anointed and appointed in his mandate to restore God's presence, he became familiar with that which is *holy*. He tried to fulfil the vision in his own strength and with carnal reasoning. When we do it our way, it can be dangerous. When we do dumb stuff outside the leading of God's presence, we open ourselves up to death, as it was in Uzzah's case. David's leadership in the flesh caused very serious repercussions for His people.

THE SHAKING TO BRING ALIGNMENT AND BIRTH THE MANDATE

In this hour, God is causing the oxen to stumble on the mandates of the flesh. He has brought His David leadership to the threshing floor before this new era is birthed, before this new move breaks forth, and He is sifting and separating the chaff from the wheat. He is shaking what can be shaken, that which is not in alignment with Him and is causing His sons and daughters to return to the fear of the Lord.

Now I can imagine David in modern terms would be referred to as a revivalist or something to that effect. A man whose heart was first and foremost for the presence of God. But he failed in his first attempt because of a lack of reverence and fear of the Lord.

THE BIRTHING OF A NEW ERA ~ BRINGING THE ARK TO JERUSALEM TAKE TWO

After sulking for a period of three months, because of God's response to his lack of reverence, David decided he would try again and fulfill the mandate God had given him of bringing the Ark back to Jerusalem. This time he decided to do it according to *God's way*. The significant change in his heart was evident in his attire. There was a display of abandoned humility before the Lord. It wasn't a professional show that would exalt him and his kingdom. No! Now he decided to strip off his earthly, kingly robes which identified his title and position, and minister unto the Lord in the priestly garment, a white linen ephod. He pointed the people's attention to the Lord in worship rather than draw attention to himself by a grand procession. This outward demonstration of the inward change in his heart is a prophetic representation of a leadership worthy of restoring and birthing this new era of God's presence among the people.

ABANDONED LOVERS

David's abandoned, radical worship is a model that the Lord requires of those desiring to walk in the Davidic government. The Lord yearns and calls for a people who will worship Him in Spirit and in truth. This is the model of the restoration of the presence. God is inviting emerging leaders with the heart of David to strip themselves of traditions, formalities, expectations, performance, selfish self-seeking agendas and carnal reasonings and to be baptized afresh in His fire. For the Lord is seeking an abandoned love, transparent and raw, authentic of heart, immersed in the fear of the Lord. This devotion to the fear of God instead of the fear of man, results in a people worshipping the KING with a radical abandoned love. A love on display and not hidden behind reputation and status, dignity and tradition. A love that catches like wild fire and calls the people of God to follow suit.

FRESH FIRE TO LIGHT THE WICKS OF HEARTS

The Lord is aligning hearts in this season, like in the days of Elijah when He was the God who answered by fire! We are in those days where the Lord is going to reveal Himself to His people by fire! For it wasn't the world the Lord was trying to convince, but a people called by His name, diseased by idolatry and witchcraft.

As Elijah rebuilt the altar in 1 Kings 18, so the altar of the heart is now being restored and aligned. The foundation of the Kingdom government is being relayed, prophetically represented by Elijah placing the 12 stones as he rebuilt the altar. And as Elijah poured water over the altar before the fire from heaven consumed it, so hearts are being immersed in the waters of repentance before the baptism of fire may consume it.

That is the shaking part, the threshing floor, a fresh circumcision of the heart, the trimming of the wick in Matthew 25. The wicks of our hearts need to be trimmed, where revelation once burned, where we knew and did things a certain way, God is calling us into a *new way*. We need to cut off the old way of doing things by trimming the wick, a fresh repentance of the heart. He is coming with fresh fire and fresh fire won't burn on an old wick. He wants us to burn with fresh revelation because He is taking us in a way we have never been before (Joshua 3:4). Let's allow Him to pour the water over the altar of our hearts and be baptized afresh in the Jordan of repentance.

There needs to be a fresh circumcision of the heart, a fresh cutting back of the flesh from the realm of sense and reason, the place of doing things in the arm of the flesh because God is calling us higher. Now is the season of the pouring of water on the altar. Embrace the refining and repent of those things that God is putting His finger on. Things that may have been ok in the last season but are not in the next. Now you are in a time of preparation for the fresh fire.

Now is the season to be baptized afresh in the FEAR OF THE LORD and to remember it is not by might, nor by power but by His spirit (Zechariah 4:6).

This fresh fire encapsulates the fear of the Lord. The fear of the Lord will cause you to depart from evil and enable you to walk in His light and His wisdom (Proverbs 9:10). The fear of the Lord will mark the separate ones, who will not partake in the corruption of this world.

THE FEAR OF THE LORD RETURNING TO THE CHURCH

The word of the Lord came to me saying;

"The fear of the Lord is returning to My people, to My leaders that have the heart of David but need an adjustment and alignment to do things MY WAY, just like David with his failed first attempt putting the ark on the wagon. The fear of the Lord is returning to My Church so that they will worship Me in a way pleasing to Me, not pleasing to man or themselves.

For what is pleasing to Me is not always pleasing to those of the household of Saul. To those who put emphasis on how the flesh looks, to those who fear man and man's opinions rather than My opinion. For Michal, Saul's daughter, mocked and held David in contempt for the worship that pleased Me (2 Samuel 6:16). Those of the house of carnality will mock, and will despise that which pleases Me. For the mind of the flesh is at war with the mind of the Spirit (Romans 8). For what pleases Me may be offensive to the carnal mind. But to those who have aligned their heart in this season and who have repented like David for trying to carry that which is holy in an unholy way, to those who have poured the water of repentance on the altar of their hearts and say "SEND YOUR FIRE, WE NEED YOUR FRESH FIRE LORD!", I will display my pleasure of such a sacrifice, and I will answer by FIRE, and it will be seen who serves me in purity and righteousness by the manifest FIRE OF MY PRESENCE IN THEIR MIDST.

On those who strip themselves of the cloak of dignity and the approval addiction of man, I will pour out My favor, I will raise them up as a voice in the land that I will send them. In the land that I will send them, they shall be My light burning bright in the midst of the night! They will be My torches, they will be My beacons of truth. For those that choose to worship Me in Spirit and in truth and worship around the right altar, I will meet with FIRE.

For even in the days of David, where there was a procession of great praise and worship leading the ark on the "new wagon", It was not met with My endorsement or favor. And even so in the days of Elijah, the prophets of Baal worshipped around a false altar, all sacrificing, cutting themselves and making a lot of "noise", but it did not attract My fire. All the noise in the world at church does not mean that I have arrived, for you will know because I am a God who answers by FIRE!

Know this is the hour of the Davids who will strip themselves of earthly reputation, titles and the need to be looked upon with respect, awe and honor, and become transparent before Me.

135

This is the new breed of leadership. This is the new government. Who don't fear to be vulnerable and expose their weaknesses and shortcomings, who are honest and don't hide behind the cloak of respectability and reputation.

The house of Saul (the flesh) seeks honor, respect, admiration, praise, reputation, but those of the house of David (the Spirit) say I AM ENOUGH!"

We know David faced persecution from those closest to him. David's own wife (Saul's daughter) mocked and scorned his undignified self-abandoned worship before the Lord. His response to her was; "watch me, I'll go even lower than this, in order for my King to be lifted higher!"

This Kingdom Government that is emerging will lift Him high. Not the name of organizations, churches, ministries or programs. They will lift Him high and then we will see all men drawn unto Him!

Chapter 8

THE DAVIDIC GOVERNMENT

Throughout the journey of writing this book and carrying this message, I have had some profound encounters that have prophesied this shift of government taking place in the Body of Christ.

Many times, my life as a prophet is metaphorical and circumstances in the natural prophesy what the Lord is doing or going to do with His people in that season.

NEW ORDER, NEW CAR, NEW WINE AND DAVID'S LOST KEYS ARE FOUND!

In the month of November 2018, the Lord led me to gather my close intercessors to fast and pray, because He announced to me that November would mark a shift, moving into December, the 12th month, symbolizing an establishment of divine government.

Leading up to the fast, I was led to 1 Samuel chapter 1 which describes the story of Hannah, Samuel's mother, who after experiencing years of barrenness, found herself in deep distress inconsolably crying out to the Lord for His hand to move on her behalf. The story goes on to share that Eli (the high priest at that time in Israel) finds her weeping and asks her what is troubling her soul. She openly and vulnerably shares the deep sorrow of her situation. To her surprise, she finds favour in Eli's sight and he prophesies that her heart's desire will soon be met.

The story goes on and exactly that happened. However, in Hannah's distressful moment, she pledges to the Lord that she would offer this son to the Lord to serve the Lord in the temple all the days of his life.

This baby that Hannah conceived and gave birth to, is as we know the famous prophet Samuel, who represented a new order of government in that day. Eli the current priest at the time, had turned a blind eye to his rebellious, harlot sons who were defiling that which was holy in the temple, making a mockery of the very sacred role of the priesthood.

My story continues…. As the week rolled on leading up to the fast, circumstantial encounters began to manifest, signposting the hand of God moving in this governmental shift.

A few days before the fast, I received a new car that I had been believing the Lord for. The brand, the colour, everything was sovereignly provided by God, again another prophetic, strategic circumstantial outplay of a prophetic picture. You see, the Lord told me months earlier, *"Anita when your new car manifests, it will be a marker of a new season, a new vehicle for a new season."* The interesting thing is, the Lord showed me months earlier the colour and the brand He wanted me to believe Him for. Normally I wouldn't choose a car of that particular colour, but somehow the desire was deposited into my heart. The colour was deep wine red, and the brand of the car was a Jeep "Compass". The Lord had been giving me dreams about new wine and before long I found myself literally obsessed with this wine colour. I had to decorate my house in this colour, I had to buy clothes in this colour, all to prophesy this new wine for this new season. This new outpouring from a new wineskin, a new order.

So, this car manifested suddenly, out of the blue, everything I had in my heart with all the extra trimmings. Then I realised the name of the car was also prophetic, a Jeep "Compass". The Lord, through this prophetic story playing out in my life, was declaring that in this season He is not only releasing new wine from a new order through a new vehicle, but is also giving us the compass (the navigation) how to follow Him in this new season. Mind blowing seriously!

Well you might be asking, "what has that got to do with Samuel, the new order?" Track with me, it gets better.

So, I go and register the car and change the ownership into my name on the 22nd of November (yes, the date is significant), not planning or thinking anything of it by the way. And as I go to the personnel counter, I look at the lady's name serving me, her name is HANNAH!! Coincidence? I don't think so! The Lord was confirming that it all linked up to the intercessory fast and the manifestation of the new vehicle. But it gets better!!!

The guy's name we bought the Jeep from (all in this strategic week, now remember, leading up to the fast of Hannah) is, yep you guessed it, DAVID! Now an uncanny thing happened with the purchase exchange of this car. David, who is an unbelieving Chinese national studying in Australia, brought his beautiful girlfriend with him to do the exchange. When they returned home to their house after dropping the car off, he discovered he had lost his house keys! He calls my husband's cell phone and kindly asks him to have a thorough look in the car to see if he can locate his house keys. My husband looks very thoroughly even under the spare tire cover, but no keys. He informs a very distressed David that we do not have his house keys.

In the meantime, our intercession team and I began the fast. The first night of our prayer gathering was more than profound, to put it lightly. Time and unction don't permit me to reveal all details of what was birthed in the intercession session regarding our specific pursuit of God in this season, but one thing I can mention, was a significant occurrence and encounter with the Spirit of God in our midst, which signified the coming forth of the new order, the shift of government that He revealed in the lead up to the fast.

That same night, we receive a text message from David, saying, "I don't mean to be offensive, but may I please come and look for the keys myself, as I have a stone in my heart that cannot be overturned". My husband by this stage is clicking on that this is the Lord. My husband always has a nose for a ripe soul and had mentioned to me upon meeting David initially that he thought the Lord had brought them across our path to share the gospel with them.

As my husband was on a salvation tangent (which I witnessed to by the way), and I was on a prophetic tangent, my eyes and ears were opened to something so profound it blew my mind. I was on the phone to my close friend and intercession partner, discussing the different occurrences in our intercession gathering the night before, when my husband interrupted and said, "David will be here at such and such time." I then relayed to my friend on the phone what was going on and what came out of my mouth stopped me in my tracks as it was like I heard the sentence echo three times after I said it. I said to her, "David has lost his keys and is coming to look for them." Startled, I asked her, "Did you hear that?" I said it again, "David has lost his keys and is coming to look for them!" I said to my friend, "I cannot believe this, the Lord is showing us something so very profound."

Let me take you back to when the Lord had me register my car on the 22nd. 22 is a symbol of the key of David, government authority, reigning on earth as it is in heaven. We briefly touched on this in chapter 1.

> *And the key of the house of David I will lay upon his shoulder; he shall open and no one shall shut, he shall shut and no one shall open (Isaiah 22:22).*

This is the same day I saw the clerk named Hannah, and the Lord said to me, "*I had you take ownership of the car on the 22nd because it symbolised a door I had opened to this new season, that no man can shut.*"

Now keeping that in mind, let's continue with the story and find out what happened to David who had lost his keys. Can you see where I am going with this?

So, I am on the phone to my friend and I say the Lord is showing me something prophetic in this whole situation. I told her, "This is all in alignment with the shift of government and the birthing of the new order. The Lord is saying that the Church has misplaced the key of David that Jesus gave her in Matthew 16:19. She hasn't been walking in the government of the Kingdom, but the Lord is causing the Church to find her keys - the Key of David. This symbolises the Church awakening to the realisation of the authority and government given to her through Jesus' death, burial and resurrection." I said to her, "let us pray." So, we prayed that the angels would retrieve David's keys and he would find them, which would be a sign and confirmation that this indeed was a prophetic message coming from heaven in this season. We also prayed for his salvation as well.

So, David arrives a little later, and looking through from my lounge room window, I watch my husband interact with him and his girlfriend out on our driveway. I can't hear the conversation, but I see a lot of jumping, hugging, smiling and laughing. I wonder what is going on? I continue doing my chores. Time passes and I realise my husband is out there with them for quite a while.

Finally, he comes inside, totally elated and says, "You will never believe what happened!!!" I asked hopefully, "David found his keys?" He said "YES!! He lifted up the boot and they were right there in front of them! They weren't there the other night when I looked!" I said, "I know, the angels brought them there to signify and prophesy to the Church that the Lord has restored the keys of government back into her possession. She has again found her place, her authority, that which she had been given and put aside for many generations, has been restored!"

Let me tell you folks, I cannot even begin to describe the level of tangible glory that manifested during this conversation. My husband and I sat down at the table literally in awe of God and of the wonder of who He is.

Then my husband proceeded to tell me how he shared the gospel with David and his girlfriend Geenie. He told him it was the Lord who caused him to feel like he had a "stone in his heart that couldn't be turned", so he would come and hear the good news of the gospel. David mentioned he had Christian friends in Singapore, but had never understood Christianity. He received the gospel with joy and allowed my husband to pray for him and his girlfriend. They both powerfully experienced the presence of God and even though they didn't outwardly by confession give their hearts to Jesus right there in that moment, we know that the Lord had used this situation of him losing and finding his keys to unlock his own heart toward hearing the good news of the gospel, which will bear the fruit of salvation.

The Lord never ceases to blow my mind! He is so creative in how He tells His story and delivers a message to earth. This is the time where the Church is going to discover and uncover the authority that has already been given, but has been misplaced through religion, tradition and man partnering with demonic ideologies to unlock the realm of the spirit as did Saul in his encounter with the witch of Endor (1 Sam 28). There has been a wineskin of the house of Saul in the government of the Church who are responsible for misplacing the keys. Like Saul the old king of Israel, they too are responsible for walking in the arm of the flesh instead of the spirit.

For the Davidic government prophesies a kingdom that rules, not by might nor by power but *by His Spirit* (Zechariah 4:6).

The word of the Lord came to me regarding the shifting of government.

"Now! says the Lord, will my Church walk in the government of the Kingdom of Heaven, as the key of David of governing authority is in the hands of the new order. For I have waited for such a time. I have waited for the time that I would cause a shift of government from the House of Saul to the House of David. I have waited for such a time for the wineskin to be renewed and for the season where my Davids who have been prepared in the wilderness, are ready to rise and take their place and lead a people in the Government of the Kingdom, rather than the government of man!"

If you remember my story correctly, the night before in intercession, the Spirit of God manifested significantly in our midst through travail among other things, signifying the coming forth of the new order, the shift of government. All who were present that night can testify to this. As previously noted, I have been prophesying this new government for some years now, but there is a difference when you know it is birthed compared to just declared. The keys of the kingdom could not be restored until the new order had been birthed, because the Lord was not going to give the keys to the old order.

It is no coincidence that the event of the keys being found were the very next day. This is what the Lord talks about signs and wonders following the message (Mark 16:20).

THE DAVIDIC GOVERNMENT ~ APOSTOLIC GOVERNMENT LEADING THE CHURCH INTO VICTORY AND UNITY

The Davidic government expresses the face of the Lion of Judah which is the apostolic Church. The Lord is restoring in this hour true apostolic leadership in the Body of Christ which will bring her forth into the unity and maturity of faith (Ephesians 4). David united Israel under one king and so this apostolic government will bring the Church into the unity of faith.

Along with the role of teaching the Body of Christ how to access the realm of the Spirit and govern from heaven, apostles play a father role in the Church. One role of a father in an earthly family is to affirm the identity of the children. With the lack of apostolic government in the Body of Christ, we have seen an orphan mindset continue to manifest in the spiritual lives of believers. This orphan mindset breeds competition and rivalry, and aborts any possibility of true unity. True unity is not a paradigm whereby we all agree on every topic, but where we honor each other's differences, knowing we are incomplete without all bodily members functioning successfully.

As you remember in Chapter 6, the Lord spoke to me very clearly and said, "*Anita, true unity will manifest where sonship is demonstrated*". I had to think about that for a little while to understand what Father was saying to me. He said, "*When you believe you are an orphan, you cannot act as a son.*"

To be a son or daughter is to know who you are in Christ and to be affirmed in His identity. An orphan continually strives and seeks to find identity in other things apart from Christ. This could be their giftings, callings, talents, relationships, careers, money etc., the list could just go on and on. The sad thing is that the orphan mindset has become too common in the Body of Christ because true apostolic fathering and governing has been missing at large. Leaders with an orphan mindset place value in their position, reputation, calling, favor and affirmation of man, which in turn has caused them to value their identity based on their successes or failures or the opinions of others. The problem is that they pass this mentality on to the people they lead, breeding a competitive spirit of rivalry and strife among one another instead of working together. This has aborted the mission of the Church.

What is the mission you ask? Well, it is for Jesus to be lifted up so that all men may be drawn unto Him (John 12:32). The issue with an orphan minded government leading the Body of Christ is that the focus comes off Jesus and onto themselves. It becomes all about them, because they are seeking to find fulfillment and identity in their achievements instead of the person of Christ. They lift up their churches, ministries and their own achievements rather than lifting up the name of Christ who is the center of it all. This creates the monster of a performance culture, which is the perfect breeding ground for a religious spirit who delights in upholding the external appearance and the reliance on natural strength in the pursuit of the recognition of man. Sadly, this orphan mindset keeps the Lord's people as children and spiritually stunted.

Sonship is the complete opposite. When our identity is in Christ and our reliance and trust is in His strength, we are subject to His authority and leadership, and manifest humility. *Humility is the mark of the spiritually mature.*

The Lord once said to me,

> *"Anita, humility is knowing who you are. It is not some false sense of weakness, but rather a clear revelation of who you are. When you know who you are, you know who you are without Me."*

I know without Him, I am a sinner fallen from grace, whose righteousness apart from being found in Jesus Christ was and always will be filthy rags. It takes humility to accept and know that I am loved because He first loved me and not because of anything I can do or be. I can never be good enough in my own righteousness. I am good enough because He is. If we are continually striving for approval, acceptance, identity and affirmation, we have not yet received His righteousness and identity. Our identity is found in Christ.

So now going back to what the Lord spoke to me regarding unity. Unity will manifest where sonship is demonstrated. Why? Because when we know who we are, we don't need to strive and compete with our neighbor, nor copy the church or worship team down the road to be pleasing to the Father. These things are only done to be pleasing to man. When we are content with the authenticity of our makeup given by our Maker, we can celebrate each other's authenticity and expression of heaven. Even if we are very different, we understand that we need each other to complete the full picture of the Church rising up in her true identity and destiny.

> *For because of Him the whole body (the church in its various parts), closely joined and firmly knit together by the joints and ligaments with which it is supplied, when each part is working properly [in all its functions], grows to full maturity, building itself up in love (Ephesians 4: 16).*

Another word for unity is harmony. For example, an orchestra must flow in complete harmony with every instrument playing its part, to execute the entire music piece successfully. The instruments don't all play at the same time, some sound better together while others play on their own. The piece would be ruined if the cello all of a sudden decided to play the piano's part and the violins decided to play the flute's part. This is called dissonance or lack of agreement. When there is lack of agreement or dissonance, the purpose or overall goal is disrupted. The goal is aborted when we break rank, when we try to be someone we are not, or not yet!

Sometimes God gives us a picture of what we look like in the future and we strive to make it happen now. But then, we are in dissonance to God's plan for our lives, and abort or hinder the future from coming to pass. The key is to stay in harmony/unity/agreement with what God is doing now, with what He expects of us now. He will finish the work that He has started in us and make us what we ought to be, as long as we stick to His program and schedule (1 Peter 5:10).

When the Church is operating from a sonship mindset, they receive authentic unique assignments from heaven and the Kingdom of God advances on earth. But when we are all trying to clone ourselves after another successful ministry, we miss our mandate for the piece of Kingdom apportioned to us. This lets the body down as a whole because we all need to fulfil our individual visions.

An apostolic government equips the Church to fulfil their destiny by affirming their identity in Christ. A Church under an apostolic government will not only understand who they are in Christ, but they will also understand the authority of the Kingdom available to them.

They will dream dreams and give birth to the promises of God that are impossible to achieve by natural means. They will receive unique assignments within the seven mountains of society and we will see the nations taken for Jesus as they go into all the world preaching the gospel and making disciples. We will see the advancement of the Church like never before as this Davidic Apostolic Government takes its place in the Body of Christ in this hour.

DAVIDIC GOVERNMENT IS OF THE SPIRIT ~ PRESENCE-CENTRED, LOVERS OF GOD

Truly the passion and priority for intimacy in the Lord's presence is the main marker of a Davidic government. Those leaders the Lord is putting in office throughout the Body of Christ with a Davidic mantle will restore intimacy and the pursuit of His presence back as the *highest priority* for believers.

A Davidic government is centred around the presence of God. We see that David sought and delighted in the presence of God, and even in the midst of his many shortcomings, would always desperately yearn for/seek His presence as a vital necessity. David penned many Psalms, revealing his passion and love for the Lord's presence and his deep desire to never be cast away from it (Psalm 42:1, Psalm 51:11, Psalm 84:10, Psalm 23:6).

David was persecuted, mocked, scorned and beguiled with all kinds of judgements and jealousies for his abandoned pursuit of the Lord's presence, but he positioned himself in defiance with the attitude, "I don't care because I am a lover of God". This is an example of the new governmental heart. He was king, a person in authority but also a lover of God. As these leaders come into their true positions with their hearts aligned with God's heart, they will produce after themselves a people of God that are lovers of God.

Presence-centred government brings the Church into a place of victory because they are walking the Isaiah 61 mandate of glorifying the Lord. They place reliance on the Spirit of God and not on the works and rituals of traditions and systems.

> *Now the Lord is Spirit, and where the Spirit of the Lord is, there is freedom (2 Corinthians 3:17).*

Where the Spirit of the Lord manifests there is freedom. Let's take a look at what this freedom looks like which is spelled out for us in Isaiah 61.

> *The Spirit of the Lord God is upon me, because the Lord has anointed and qualified me to preach the Gospel of good tidings to the meek, the poor, and afflicted; He has sent me to bind up and heal the broken hearted, to proclaim liberty to the [physical and spiritual] captives and the opening of the prison and of the eyes to those who are bound, To proclaim the acceptable year of the Lord [the year of His favor] and the Day of vengeance of our God, to comfort all who mourn, To grant [consolation and joy] to those who mourn in Zion - to give them an ornament of beauty for ashes, the oil of joy instead of mourning, the garment [expressive] of praise instead of a heavy, burdened, and failing spirit - that they may be called oaks of righteousness [lofty, strong, and*

magnificent, distinguished for uprightness, justice, and right
standing with God], the planting of the Lord that He may be
glorified
(Isaiah 61:1-3).

WOW!!

These things will take place when the Spirit of the Lord is upon the Church. Where the Spirit of the Lord is, we see the Church preaching the gospel, hearts being healed, eyes being opened, folks getting free of demonic strongholds, comfort poured out on those who have experienced sorrow, joy restored, afflicted lives made new, depression lifted, songs of praises and victory released and lives established in Christ, bringing forth glory to His name! No wonder the enemy has sought to keep the Church religion focused rather than presence focused. The Lord only gets glorified through His people when we are presence focused!

I like Barbara Yoda's address to the leadership in the Body of Christ,

> *"We need to stop worrying about the needs of the people and*
> *be concerned with loving God, when we put Him first, He*
> *will meet the needs of the people."*

This is so true, if we remain focused on loving God and His presence, He will meet the needs of His people.

There is a shift in government in the House of God from those who oppose God like Saul to those who are "lovers of God" like David. There's a generation of the "lovers of God" emerging in this hour. The "lovers of God" will love not their own lives even unto death because they want to serve Him and run after Him with their whole heart. A Davidic government will give birth to the overcomer.

And they overcame him by the blood of the lamb and by the
word of their testimony; and they loved not their lives unto
the death (Revelation 12:11 KJV)

There is a cost to being presence-centred. It will cost you YOUR WAY!

Davidic governmental leaders abandon themselves to His will and His way and will pay any price for the sake of His Kingdom. They will lay down their reputation even at the cost of looking like a fool so that the presence of God will be made manifest in and among His people. This is what David did when he danced before the Ark as it was being restored to Jerusalem. This is a true shepherd with the heart of David.

From this place of His divine presence, a Davidic Government will see the Church being led by the Spirit of God which will bring forth the manifestation of the sons of God! (Romans 8:14)

INTIMACY AND PRESENCE OVER POWER AND REPUTATION

This new order is relationship and intimacy based, releasing victory from a true kingdom government.

There must have been a significant difference between Saul and David, for the Lord to take the government from Saul and give it to David, and for David to be called a man after God's own heart.

How come David had a heart after God and Saul didn't? Didn't David make more mistakes than Saul? The difference was David's repentant heart. Saul on the other hand, was stubborn and rebellious, and refused to change. He sought to please man and serve his own selfish needs over serving and pleasing God. We see this take place in 1 Samuel 13:1-24, where Saul displayed great irreverence for the order of God, making an unlawful sacrifice before the people in fear of their reproach against him.

I enjoy a post on worthychristianforums.com on Saul's unrepentant heart. They write:

"Saul displayed an unrepentant heart by first acting like nothing was wrong when Samuel confronted him, then he blame-shifted ("the men" wanted to keep the animals) then he justified his actions by claiming the disobedience was for the sake of worshipping the Lord! In other words, Saul didn't repent he was just sorry he got caught."[1]

After a series of events, Saul's house eventually came down and David's kingdom was established.

THE SAUL GOVERNMENT IS OF THE FLESH ~ SELF-CENTERED, LOVERS OF SELF

Saul represents a government appointed by man, that is self-serving and operates in the fear of man (1 Samuel 8, 1 Samuel 13).

Under the government of the flesh (Saul's house), leaders promote religion, tradition and man-made ideals, denying the Lord's people access to His presence. We saw in the earlier chapter that throughout the entire reign of Saul, the Ark of the Covenant (presence of God), was hidden away. Hidden out of sight from the people.

*But know this that in the last days perilous times will come. For men will be lovers of themselves, lovers of money, boasters, proud, blasphemous, disobedient to parents, unthankful, unholy, unloving, unforgiving, slanderers, without self-control, brutal, despisers of good, traitors, headstrong, haughty, **lovers of pleasure rather than lovers***

> *of God, having a form of Godliness but denying the power*
> *(2 Timothy 3:1 emphasis added).*

Saul had a form of godliness, but he rebelled and rejected the Word of the Lord. For this reason, Samuel said to him rebellion is as the sin of witchcraft in 1 Samuel 15:23. He didn't say rebellion was witchcraft, but he said it was the *same* as witchcraft, meaning you are serving another, and in most cases, it is *self*. Those who promote man's agenda above the Lord's, are lovers of self rather than lovers of God.

Galatians 5:19-20 lists witchcraft as one of the works of the flesh. This in essence is exaltation and service of man's will and agenda, rather than God's.

Romans 8:6-8 states that:

> *Now the mind of the flesh [which is sense and reason*
> *without the Holy Spirit] is death [death that comprises all*
> *the miseries arising from sin, both here and hereafter]. But*
> *the mind of the [Holy] Spirit is life and [soul] peace [both*
> *now and forever]. [That is] because the mind of the flesh*
> *[with its carnal thoughts and purposes] is* **hostile** *to God,*
> *for it does not submit itself to God's Law; indeed it cannot.*
> *So then those who are living the life of the flesh [catering*
> *to the appetites and impulses of their carnal nature] cannot*
> *please or satisfy God, or be acceptable to Him (emphasis*
> *added).*

So, we see here that those who follow the realm of sense and reason actually stand against the Lord. Like Saul they are sadly in rebellion to God. A life that is void of the Holy Spirit's leading, will be in rebellion to God period. Because such a person seeks to gratify the flesh rather than the Spirit of God which is not acceptable to the Lord.

Saul's Kingdom was torn from him as prophesied by Samuel because of his disobedience and willingness to fear man and preserve his own reputation rather than fear God and obey His commands.

Arrogance and pride entered Saul's heart and protecting his reputation was more important than performing the will of the Lord. He was deceived to think he was above reproof and correction. James 4:6 NKJV says:

> *The Lord resists the proud but gives grace to the humble.*

God resisted Saul and He took his anointing from him and gave it to David.

TO BE PRESENCE-CENTERED IS TO BE WORSHIP-CENTERED

As we are all aware, worship is one of the main signatures of David's life and is a marking factor to his style of *presence*-centred government. Anyone seeking presence-centred government will not be able to take one step forward without worship being the key factor. According to David's Psalms the way to enter the Lord's presence is through thanksgiving, praise and worship (Psalm 100:4, Psalm 22:3).

Worshipping in Spirit and Truth ~ A New Expression of Worship Unlocking Heaven

> *A time will come, however, indeed it is already here, when the true (genuine) worshipers will worship the Father in spirit and in truth (reality); for the Father is seeking just such people as these as His worshippers. God is Spirit (a spiritual Being) and those who worship Him **must** worship Him in Spirit and in truth (reality) (John 4:23-24 emphasis added).*

Heaven's realms are available for us to tap into when we leave behind our performed worship and enter into a place of Spirit-led worship. This verse clearly says, "God is Spirit, and those who worship Him *must* worship Him in Spirit and truth." The Lord is outlining to us *how* we are to come to him.

To worship in "Spirit" and "truth" actually means to worship, "by" the Spirit from a "genuine" place. It doesn't only mean to worship in our heavenly language, which is one aspect of worship in the Spirit that takes you into a realm of unlocking mysteries and realms of glory. We will get into that in a moment.

But to worship "by" the Spirit also means being led by Him in our worship sets even though we have a planned song set list. We give the reigns over to the Holy Spirit and say, "Lord have Your way, how You want to be worshipped today." As a worship leader myself I am aware that you need to plan your song set list, but we must also allow Holy Spirit to direct that set list as He wills. Proverbs 16:9 says:

> *A man's mind plans his way, but the Lord directs His steps*
> *and makes them sure.*

This scripture is my anchor when it comes to worship leading. I plan out my way prayerfully being led by the Holy Spirit, but during worship, I hand over the directorship to the Holy Spirit whom I follow as my conductor.

Sometimes He will land on a song and have us prophetically sing off that song before we go to the next. At other times He will land on the first song and we take off in the Spirit and do not do the rest of the set list.

Spirit-led worship is step one to worshipping in the Spirit. Now the problem with this type of worship, which is by the way, how the Lord says we *must* worship Him, is that it interferes with our schedules and time frames on the worship part of the service.

This is the biggest problem right here to why the presence of God isn't flowing in our corporate gatherings. We have restrictions on worship, and we don't follow the Lord's brief in *how* He *requires* us to worship Him.

John 4:23-24 does not say that we are to worship Him by perfect, professional songs, or smoke machines and disco lights. Please hear my heart, I'm not saying if you have those things that your worship isn't anointed. I am merely trying to provoke the reader to questio–n the foundation, reliance and place from which they worship. Do we rely on professionalism or do we rely on the leading of the Holy Spirit? The Holy Spirit knows how He desires to be worshipped, so we must surrender to His leading, and as we surrender to His leading, we will lead the people of God into the presence of God via Spirit and truth.

The question worship leaders and worship teams must pose to themselves is, who are we trying to please? God or man? Who are we trying to reach in worship, God or man? Worship shouldn't be used as a tool to perform and display a show, but instead express the heart's desire to meet with the King.

The second aspect of worship the Lord requires according to John 4:24, is to worship in "truth". Truth means reality, or in other words, authentically worshipping from a genuine heart to simply seek *His face* and to *know Him*. There are no hidden agendas, nor self-promoting motives or ambitions. It is not a performed, plastic, place of entertainment. People can go to a concert or their local pub down the road if they want to be entertained. Worship is the access point to the presence of God and must be treated as such. The Lord lands on genuine, authentic worship. I have seen the Lord's presence fall in power and glory where there was only one worship leader on a guitar. No band, no lights, not even a sound system, just a heart that was positioned in love and adoration for the Father.

Therefore, Jesus had to spell out in John 4:23-24, how the Father desires to be worshipped. It is from a place of pure undefiled expression seeking to exalt the Lord and the Lord alone. Not to draw attention to yourself or perform and show off for the praises of man. This is not the kind of worship that the Lord requires or even desires for that matter.

Now I would like to explain the second step to worshipping in the Spirit which contains the power to unlock heaven in ways we have yet to experience.

A few years ago, I had a vision of corporate worship. I saw the saints worshipping together in the Spirit with one heart and mind. I mean they were worshipping the Father in their heavenly language (tongues). As the corporate worship shifted from a natural language to the heavenly language a "pulling" began to happen. A "pulling on heaven" and a vertical portal was created, and as the worship in tongues went up, I saw the mysteries of heaven coming down. The mysteries that were being unlocked were needed for that particular gathering. And mysteries were imparted to each individual gathered in that place at that time. As each person worshipped in their heavenly language, they were unlocking their own hearts and were entering into a liberty they had not known before. It truly was spirit to Spirit communion and an unhindered flow as the worship went up, the mysteries came down. Answers, revelations, encounters, miracles of all kinds, were taking place as the worship in the Spirit created an atmosphere of intimacy, freedom and victory. As the mysteries were being released, it truly was like tapping into heaven and bringing it on earth.

You Can't Unlock Heaven With The Arm Of The flesh.

I saw how limited natural worship was (even though it does access a realm of glory), but that alone is not going to suffice in these days to come. When we worship in our heavenly language it is spirit to Spirit, because God is Spirit and John 4 says He *requires* us to worship Him spirit to Spirit. Our own efforts, striving, or professionalism are not going to access and unlock the realms of heaven needed for the *demonstration* of the Kingdom in this time.

The Greater Glory

The realms of glory and heaven the Lord desires to release in these days require a greater level of access to the mysteries of heaven so His Kingdom can come in greater dimensions than ever before.

There is a greater glory to be unlocked and unleashed on earth and as we worship Him in spirit (our heavenly language), in one accord in our meetings, we are going to see heaven explode in our midst.

Again, the problem the Church faces with this particular expression of worship, is that it challenges our systems, structures, and our concern to please man. People just need to be taught the Lord's way and they will enter into worship in the Spirit. The issue is they are so used to entertainment and the 30-minute song set, anything over that timeframe would be too long.

Let me tell you, when you forge a culture of Spirit led worship (which is currently against most church worship cultures), the people will not be able to go back to formula performed worship. Why? Because they are able to access the Lord's presence through Spirit-led worship in ways performed worship cannot. Spirit-led worship will be a key signature of this emerging Davidic Government.

FEARLESS COURAGE MARKS DAVIDIC LEADERSHIP WHO SILENCES THE VOICE OF GOLIATH

David had courage to face a giant who was intimidating one of the most able armies of his day. To fearlessly declare to a giant without wearing armor, "Who shall defy the armies of the Living God?", you would think he was either crazy or extremely brave and full of courage. To have a heart after God, courage is an essential ingredient and it is vital to walk by faith. It doesn't take courage to stay in the status quo of religion and tradition, or to remain in comfort zones. It takes courage to obey God and let the Lord have His way.

David could overcome because he was dependent on God!

A self-serving government will not lead people into victory. They will compromise at the first sign of persecution and bend to political correctness.

In order to confront Goliath, whose taunts have intimidated and paralyzed the forward advancement of God's people, fearless courage (which a self-serving government lacks) is required to confront Goliath, whose taunts have intimidated and paralyzed the advancement of God's people.

You cannot protect your reputation or be a slave to opinions/judgements of those in Saul's house, if you truly possess courage.

True victors arising are those who have died to their reputations. They will truly be a voice shaking nations as they bear "witness" by the word of their testimony of the power of the cross.

The fires of persecution will not harm or hinder them because they have been prepared in the fire of the Lord. They have been threshed and molded, pruned and prepared by the hand of the Lord.

There are people in the Body of Christ that are so desperate for Spirit-led leadership. They are fed up with dead religion and rituals. They are fed up playing church in Saul's house and desire to worship at His throne. They want a leadership that will lead them into victory.

The Davids will come forth from the chambers of intimacy knowing their God and shall do mighty exploits. From this place of intimacy, they will stand up before the enemies of God's people and declare, "Who shall defy the armies of the living God?"

This rising Davidic government will raise up an army of fearless warriors, who will take the heavens by force. They will run with the chariots like Elijah and the acceleration of God will be upon them as they run by the wind of the Spirit.

This leadership will bring the Church into the new wineskin that is self-sacrificing rather than self-serving. From this heart position the Lord's people will truly be able to overcome persecutions.

THE SOUND OF THE LION ~ THE SOUND OF VICTORY

There is a sound of victory that is going to permeate from the people of God as the Lord brings forth this new government of David.

> *Then one of the [twenty-four] elders said to me, Stop weeping! Look closely, the Lion of the tribe of Judah, the Root of David, has won he has **overcome and conquered**! (Revelation 5:5 emphasis added)*

We see here in this scripture that our own Messiah, Yeshua, the Lion of the Tribe of Judah who has triumphed, is from the *root* of David. This is key to understanding the importance of the emerging Kingdom government that is being established in the Body of Christ in this hour.

In Chapter 1 we noted the Lord saying, He is giving the keys (the key of David) to His Church, to govern and bring heaven on earth.

> *And the key of the house of David I will lay upon his shoulder; he shall open and no one shall shut, he shall shut and no one shall open (Isaiah 22:22)*

If the Church is not operating in a Davidic governmental order (of the Holy Spirit) but is still operating under a Saul order (of the flesh, sense and reason), they won't have access to these keys of authority.

As previously explained, keys represent access, ownership and authority. The Lord has given His Church the keys of the Davidic kingdom, Messiah's eternal kingdom, so they can walk in victory.

The establishment of the Davidic Kingdom Government through the Church (His redeemed), will be the manifest evidence of the King of Glory coming in! And this Kingdom Government will make way for the Avenger, the King of Glory, reigning in victory, justice and might here on earth.

Chapter 9

THE GOVERNMENT OF ESTHER

I'm prefacing this chapter to avoid confusion, the government of Esther and the metaphorical references to Esther mentioned in this chapter are by no means reserved only for women. This is a message to the *whole* Body of Christ and the characteristics of the Esther government are to be displayed in both male and female alike.

MUCH GIVEN, MUCH REQUIRED

You could say Queen Vashti was given much. She had her private royal living quarters, her own entourage of servants and handmaidens. She had access to the most expensive beautifying oils and perfumes of her time, not to mention her wardrobe!! It would have been equivalent to the top designer clothes of today and let's not for a moment forget the beautiful bedazzlement of precious jewels and diamonds she would have been accustomed to adorning herself with daily. She had a very colorful social life, as you would remember, she was having a party entertaining her friends when the King called for her. She didn't have to lift a finger, and well, could I put it this way, her life would have been very self-indulgent. She seemingly didn't respect or value the honor of her position and the riches bestowed upon her, let's say, the perks that went with being queen. She apparently failed to realize or remember that this prestigious position of Queen of Persia and the riches that accompanied the title, carried a great and weighty requirement. You see the Queen belonged to the King and the King required her obedience. On this particular day, he required her to display her *beauty* (Esther 1).

The name Vashti means "beautiful" and, she was *very* beautiful. In this time in Persia, the beauty of the queen would reflect the majesty of the king and his kingdom. Therefore, by requesting his beautiful Queen to come and display her beauty before the guests at the feast, the King was in essence showing off his most prized possession, his Queen, the *heart* of his majestic kingdom. However, her obstinate and defiant refusal to obey his request and come before his guests, tore down his honor as a husband and King and was a very humiliating slap in the face publicly before his kingdom. She was given much but she failed to fulfil her "much required".

Now before you judge this as a very harsh and disrespectful request, you must understand that Queen Vashti was very aware of her requirements as Queen before she married the King. She knew the legal and cultural expectations of her position, but she displayed a very independent, self-centred and may I even dare to say prideful attitude towards the King and the kingdom. Why do I say prideful? Because the essence of pride is assuming yourself more important than you ought. It is forgetting your position and the requirements thereof. Pride has a self-centred shield and motivation. Queen Vashti lost sight of her true position as queen and by refusing the King's command, she placed herself above him. This action of defiance stripped her of her crown, to prevent her disobedience being regarded as an acceptable example to the women of Persia, which would result in upheavals in households across the land.

And Memucan answered before the king and the princes,
Vashti the queen has not only done wrong to the King but
to all the princes and to all the peoples who are in all the
provinces of King Ahasuerus. For this deed of the queen
will become known to all women, making their husbands
contemptible in their eyes, since they will say, King Ahasuerus
commanded Queen Vashti to be brought before him, but she
did not come. This very day the ladies of Persia and Media
who have heard of the queen's behavior will be telling it to
all the king's princes. So contempt and wrath in plenty will
arise (Esther 1:16-17).

Breaking rank causes chaos. Order is maintained when position is
maintained. We see here that Vashti hadn't only done wrong to the King
but also to all those in the kingdom. Her example of rebellion would directly
result in rebellion in the homes throughout the kingdom. This is the same
in the Church. Those in positions of leadership set an example of godliness
in the house of God. When the leadership is in rebellion, it flows from the
head down.

The King was advised, for the sake of the kingdom, to strip her from her
crown and her position given to someone "better" than she.

If it pleases the king, let a royal command go forth from
him and let it be written among the laws of the Persians
and Medes, so that it may not be changed, that Vashti is to
[be divorced and] come no more before King Ahasuerus; and
let the king give her royal position to another who is better
than she (Esther 1:19).

And it was so, she was removed from her position and was replaced by
another better than she.

In chapter 2 of the book of Esther, we read that the King felt sorry afterwards for sending Vashti away. This is a prophetic picture of the Lord's heart. The Lord doesn't want to remove people, but He wants them to yield, obey and *move with Him*. He wants to display His glory through them and reward them with His favor and majesty. But for the *sake* of His people and His Kingdom, He cannot allow rebellion to rule. Vashti was in rebellion. Those who reject and resist *how* He wants to move and do things apart from His leading and ways, are sadly in rebellion.

THE VASHTI GOVERNMENT ~AN INDEPENDENT AND REBELLIOUS SPIRIT

1 Samuel 15:23 says, *"Rebellion is as the sin of witchcraft"*, and in Galatians 5:20, witchcraft is listed as a work of the flesh. Those who rebel against/ resist the move and touch of God, are in fact yielding to the flesh and are hence disempowered to produce the fruit of the Holy Spirit, which as the scripture below outlines, inhibits inheriting the Kingdom.

> *Now the work of the flesh are manifest, which are these;*
> *Adultery, fornication, uncleanness, lasciviousness, idolatry,*
> *witchcraft, hatred, variance, emulations, wrath, strife,*
> *seditions, heresies, envyings, murders, drunkenness,*
> *revellings, and such like: of which I tell you before, as I*
> *have also told you in time past that they which do such*
> *things shall not inherit the kingdom of God. But the fruit*
> *of the Spirit is love, joy, peace, longsuffering, gentleness,*
> *goodness, faith, meekness, temperance: against such*
> *there is no law. But the fruit of the Spirit is love, joy,*
> *peace, longsuffering, gentleness, goodness, faith, meekness,*
> *temperance: against such there is no law (Galatians 5:19-*
> *23 KJV).*

The Lord desires His body, His Church to produce and display the fruit of the Holy Spirit, which supersedes the dictates of this natural realm. Whereby you can have peace in the midst of a storm, joy in the midst of turmoil, patience in great conflict, faith in dire circumstances and love towards your enemies.

His fruit is His beauty, but if we are separated from the source of the fruit – the Holy Spirit, then the only other fruit that will be in operation and demonstration is the fruit of the flesh.

A rebellious and independent spirit is fuelled by carnality. This spirit's seat of operation is the realm of sense and reason and therefore when in operation, its goals and aims revolve around this realm. It focuses on what is appetizing to the flesh. It hollows a question, "What exalts my flesh and the senses thereof?" We need to understand that whatever seeks to exalt man and his needs above the needs of the Holy Spirits is not born of God. Whatever causes us to *compromise* gratifying the Holy Spirit is an enemy of God.

> *Do you not know that being the world's friend is being God's enemy? So, whoever chooses to be a friend of the world takes his stand as an enemy of God (James 4:4b).*

Seeker and world friendly churches compromise gratifying the Holy Spirit to fulfil their goal, and therefore in doing so they position themselves as an enemy of God.

Lovers of God put God and pleasing Him first, no matter the cost. And yes, there is a cost to pleasing Him first. The question is what price are you willing to pay? It might cost you your comfortability, your reputation, your finances…. *your way*. It might cost you your life!

When Jesus said in Matthew 16:24, "*If anyone desires to be My disciple, let him deny himself [disregard, lose sight of and forget himself and his own interests] and take up his cross and follow Me*", in essence He was saying, "if you are to be my true disciple, then you must lay down your life for *My* cause".

His cause is whatever destiny entails. His way, His will.

HIS WAY IS ATTACHED TO HIS WILL

Understanding that God has a "way" in performing His "will", is essential in our walk with the Lord. I was on a plane to Singapore preparing my heart for a series of meetings that I was going to do at a prophetic conference, when I began to pray, "Lord, I pray your will be done over these next few days ....etc." and then the Holy Spirit interrupted my most noble of prayers, interjecting what I think was a rhetorical question. He said,

> *"That sounds all lovely, noble and certainly spiritual Anita, but the question I have for you is, do you want My **way**?"*

He then went on to say,

> *"Many people desire My will, they want the blessed outcome in their lives and others', as My will is always good and not evil, but not everyone wants the way in which I perform My will. This is where My people can find "My way" as a stumbling block to their natural mind. It is designed this way so that you cannot perform My will in your life in your own ability, because My ways are higher than your ways and My thoughts higher than your thoughts." (Isaiah 55:9).*

Well, this just left me stunned sitting in my seat. He continued in His explanation and spoke to me about Jesus and His commission here on earth as the sacrificial Lamb for all mankind. The narrative of Jesus praying His final prayer in the garden of Gethsemane in preparation for His crucifixion, flashed through my mind (Luke 22). Jesus was fully aware of His part in fulfilling God's will by redeeming mankind and reconciling the breach caused by the high treason of Adam in the Garden of Eden. This was the will of God, a most triumphant and glorious outcome, but for a moment the "way" seemed to press so heavily upon Him that He sweated blood and uttered a prayer He immediately relented from.

> *Father if it be possible may you cause this cup, (this way)*
> *to pass by me (Luke 22:42).*

In essence, He was asking the Father not to negate His will, as Jesus' heart was to see all mankind redeemed, but it was for a moment, a plea, that maybe just maybe it could be done *another way?* He then immediately repents from this request and says, "But not My will but Yours be done". You see, you cannot have God's will without having His way. In His sacrifice, Jesus not only yielded to God's will, but He yielded to God's way in fulfilling His will.

Everyone is crying out for "revival" or to see "miracles" and the awesome demonstration of God's power. But sweet brethren, this is only reserved for those that respond to His call, and answer and obey *His* voice. This is reserved for those who will embrace His way along with His will.

What if the Spirit of God moved in a way that offended your mind? What if He decided to perform His will outside of the box we envisioned in our mind?

The alarming factors in the Body of Christ these days are the spirit of humanism gripping the minds of believers, and leaders adopting an independent attitude of being led by the voice of the natural realm of sense and reason instead of being led by the Spirit of God. We have broken rank like Vashti and exalted our way and will in our pursuits for the "Kingdom of God", only to be led by the voice of the natural. We cannot win a spiritual battle and war, and take ground for the kingdom by heeding the voice of the natural and using natural weapons (the arm of the flesh).

We put programs in place that only perform as a mask to the absence of God's presence in our churches, and worship by large around a man-made altar, making a lot of noise (and by jingoes we make that noise with an air of professionalism, don't forget that) catering to people with a taste for commercialism rather than a hunger and thirst for righteousness.

Gaining and maintaining reputation and recognition has been a silent goal in itself for many (not all) leaders in the governmental structure of the Church today. Sadly, this motivation is one of the main contributing factors to why the present-day Church, in general, is void of power. Recognition, reputation, and approval have been laid as silent motivational foundations for doing what we do in church. Why else would we seek to construct our church services around what suits and pleases the people rather than what suits and pleases the Spirit of God? When the needs of man are lifted up, the church starts to grow in attendance, there are multiple structured services a day with NO room for the Spirit of God to move, we call this a successful church! The number of people attending is not what God deems as a successful church. But whether He is attending, is what deems a church successful.

Friends awaken your ears! Let them be unstopped! There is a deep cry coming from the people of God throughout the nations of this earth for more. I believe there is now window of the Lord to repent from operating in the heart and spirit of Vashti, or else those refusing to repent will lose their seat of authority and be replaced by Esthers. The Spirit of the Lord weighs heavy on my heart as I write this, as I feel this is the key to revival in the land you are beseeching the Lord to possess. He will not share His glory with another, meaning someone with another heart. He wants to display His glory through His Church, through His people.

THE LORD REQUIRES OUR BEAUTY

The name Esther means star/bright light. The Lord has called His Church, His bride to be as Esther, one who will display His majesty and the glory of His Kingdom. One who at the King's call, will come and display her beauty, the beauty of the majesty of her King. In her obedience to the voice of her King, His splendor, majesty and power is revealed. The Lord desires to display His beauty through His Church. He has paid a high price for the demonstration of His Kingdom and the power thereof to be available to and move through His people. He not only wants this for His people, but he *requires* this. Much given much required (Luke 12:48). King Ahasuerus required Queen Vashti to display her beauty before his kingdom as a demonstration and reflection of his majesty. 1 Corinthians 11:7 says:

"Woman is the glory of the man".

The Lord is requiring His bride to display her beauty and reflect His majesty to the nations of the earth. What makes His bride beautiful? It is *His* beauty, it is *His* Glory!

Vashti, likened to the meaning of her name, was very beautiful, but she was rebellious. She was independent and taken up with her *own* glory. A Vashti church will be more concerned with making everything beautiful on the outside (beautiful stage, beautiful services, beautiful clothes, beautiful lights, beautiful seats, beautiful programs), but give no attention to the true beauty and that is the glory and presence of the King. A Vashti church will take confidence in the natural beauty and fail to heed the call of the King to display the true beauty – His presence and move of His Spirit. In order for the true beauty to be displayed, it requires complete humble surrender to the King.

HUMILITY ATTRACTS HEAVEN

Now, as a woman, I love beautiful. I like things to be pretty and beautiful in the natural. So do not misunderstand me. I am not saying to make things ugly. I am not saying to make the stage ugly or have ugly uncomfortable seats, or dress like the cat has just dragged you in! The Lord is a God of excellence and I wholeheartedly believe in displaying excellence in everything we do in service of our King. What I am saying is to not put our confidence in the external appearances (Phil 3:3). Esther had another weapon in addition to her beauty, which was something called favor! It is the grace of God! The grace and favor of God is what turned a decree of death around for her nation. It wasn't her natural beauty!

> *And it was so, when the king saw Esther the queen standing in the court, that she obtained favor in his sight: and the king held out the golden sceptre that was in his hand. So Esther drew near, and touched the top of the sceptre. Then said the king unto her, What wilt thou, queen Esther? And what is thy request? It shall be even given thee to the half of the kingdom (Esther 5:2-3 KJV).*

She found favor in his sight, which moved his heart to grant her request. This shows us that it's the favor of God that moves mountains. It is by His grace and unmerited favor that we have been set free.

> *In Him we have redemption (deliverance and salvation) through His blood, the remission (forgiveness) of our offenses (shortcomings and trespasses), in accordance with the riches and the generosity of His gracious favour (Ephesians 1:7).*

James 4:6 says that God gives grace to the humble. So, for Esther to have walked in such grace and favor, she would have had to have a surrendered, humble heart. She demonstrated this in the three day fast before her meeting with the King.

A pretty pulpit will not raise a man from the dead. A beautiful stage will not set a drug addict free. Beautiful chairs will not heal a marriage. NO!!! It is by the grace of God upon a surrendered heart, which is dead to their own life, sown as a seed in the ground and now alive through the resurrection power of the King (Matt 16:25). We, as believers, are called to a life of surrender, which is the call of the King.

Everyone who has read the book of Esther will know that she faced the call of the King of heaven, by standing in the gap for the Jewish nation (her people) and asking the King of Persia (her husband) to reverse the decree of death that he had issued because of his wicked advisor Haman. This was a great call as it required her to face death. Only those called by King Ahasuerus were allowed to present themselves before him in the royal court. (Esther 4:11).

> *For if you keep silent at this time, relief and deliverance shall arise for the Jews from elsewhere, but you and your father's house will perish. And who knows but that you have come to the kingdom for such a time as this and for this very occasion? (Esther 4:14)*

In this famous conversation between her and her cousin Mordecai, documented in Esther 4:14, he sternly and desperately encourages her that she has been placed in such a privileged position for a greater purpose outside of herself. In essence, he was telling her to respond to the call of the Lord and display His beauty. In other words, he was saying to her, "Are you going to heed the call, surrender your life, receive the beauty of His majesty that can make any wrong right? Or are you going to live for yourself, save your own life and not pay a price for the Kingdom?"

Esther's famous response to Mordecai in Esther 4:16, "If I perish, I perish", was a picture of her fully surrendered heart to the hand and will of God. This is where she was able to demonstrate the kingdom, by laying down her life for the sake of a whole nation. God can cause great shifts and breakthroughs though this level of yielding.

This same conversation is happening now from heaven to earth. This same desperate call is going forth to the Lord's people, to understand that it is not for themselves that they have been given the keys of the Kingdom. It is not for themselves that they have been given access to heaven's treasuries. But it is for the greater purpose of a generation, that so desperately needs to see the truth of the light, and the demonstration of the gospel in power, to deliver their souls from hell.

THE BOOK OF ESTHER ~ A PROPHESY TO THE END TIME CHURCH

If we look at the book of Esther with prophetic eyes, we will see that this book is a prophetic message and demonstration of the end time Church. We are in a moment in time, where a shift of government is taking place throughout the Body of Christ. It is for the "sake" of the Kingdom that the government of Vashti is being removed and a new government is taking place, the government of Esther.

We are in a time of the ages, where a similar scenario as in the book of Esther is playing out. Haman has been on the rampage long enough, releasing decrees from hell through demonic narratives that are molding our society and younger generations into an Anti-Christ belief system that will send them to hell. The Vashti church has been too interested in her own kingdom and outward beauty instead of surrendering her pride, and risking her reputation to display the Lord's beauty (glory) to the world which would shift the hold of demonic narratives on this generation, unlock the darkness and restore them into the kingdom of light.

Therefore, for the sake of the Kingdom, there is a shift of government taking place in the Church in this season from the Government of Vashti to the Government of Esther.

A PURE HEART WILL SEE GOD MOVE

Purity is what marks an Esther government. She had a pure heart with no agenda. She didn't go to the throne because she had an agenda to fulfil. She didn't have to promote herself to gain favor with the King but merely was clothed in the grace and favor of God which made her stand out and be noticed by him.

> *Blessed are the pure in heart: for they shall **see** God (Matthew 5:8 KJV emphasis added).*

This scripture literally means that those holding no other agenda than to know God and His truth shall recognize Him and stand with eyes wide open. They will see God move in His awesome wonder and recognize Him when He "shows up". They don't find it a foreign commodity when His Spirit manifests in their midst and begins to move upon His people. They hold the attitude, "Have Your way Lord, not my way but Yours".

A Vashti Government will *not* recognize a move of God's Spirit. They will *not* have eyes to see because of the pride acting as a veil over the heart.

> *The pride of your heart has deceived you (Obadiah 1:3a NKJV)*

If we remember, it was pride that veiled the hearts and eyes of the religious leaders and scribes in Jesus' time, and hindered them from seeing Him for who He really was.

The Lord is birthing a new heart in the government of His church.

> *And I will give them one heart [a new heart] and I will put a new spirit within them, and I will take the stony heart out of their flesh and will give them a heart of flesh [one that is sensitive and responsive to the touch of their God (Ezekiel 11:19).*

Those with the heart of Esther recognize and are responsive to the touch of their God. They are sensitive to the promptings and moves of the Holy Spirit and are quick to give Him room in their midst.

POSITIONED TO DEMONSTRATE THE KINGDOM OF HEAVEN

Esther was positioned in a place of influence and government to demonstrate the mandate of the Kingdom of Heaven. The Lord has called His Church, His bride to be as Esther, displaying His majesty and the glory of His Kingdom. He wants to display His glory through His Church, through His people and for them to *demonstrate* His Kingdom in *power*.

> *But you are a chosen race, a royal priesthood, a dedicated nation, [God's] own purchased, special people, that you may set forth the wonderful deeds and **display** the virtues and perfections of Him Who called you out of darkness into His marvelous light (1 Peter 2:9 emphasis added).*

This scripture clearly explains that we are called to display His glory. If you don't know your destiny or calling is in God, then this scripture is for you. You are called to demonstrate the Kingdom in the power and authority of heaven.

Esther was placed in a position of government to execute the will of God. And so, it is with His people in this hour. The Lord is positioning his people like Esther, to execute the will of God. It is not for our agenda, it is not for our purpose, but God is raising up a people like Esther to cause great generational and national shifts and victories.

ESTHER GOVERNMENT SERVES THE AGENDA OF THE KING OF HEAVEN

Promotion is not just about us, but it is a place where service is demonstrated. As I said earlier, privileged position is for a greater purpose outside of yourself.

Esther was not put in a strategic position of influence just to look pretty, but to serve a higher agenda. It was the King of Heaven's agenda. The Lord's agenda is always for the good of His people. And so, the heart of an Esther government is to serve the greater good of the people even at the cost of laying down their own lives to accomplish it.

Esther in her royal position was required to give of herself for the sake of the people – even if it cost her, her life.

CALLED TO EXECUTE JUSTICE

Remember, the name Esther means bright/light, which is a prophetic picture of the end time Church shining bright with the glory of the Lord. So bright that nations will come to that light (Isaiah 60:1). Not only that, but also for the purpose of light exposing darkness.

We read in Esther 2:21-23, that evil strategies and plans were immediately revealed the moment she was placed in her governmental position. The plot against the King's life, and then in later chapters the evil plan of Haman to annihilate the Jews.

When the devil is exposed, justice can be executed.

Only when the root of the enemy's plan is hidden, can he continue to wreak havoc in our lives.

We are in an hour in the church age where the Church is rising with the light and the glory of God, like Esther, exposing the plans and strategies of the devil to execute justice and vengeance, bringing a mighty turning of the tables.

The two who had plotted to kill the King were hanged, as well as Haman who was later on exposed (Esther 2:23, Esther 7:10).

This narrative in Esther is a prophetic picture of the justice of God being executed through the Avenger, the King of Glory, as the governmental shifts happen, allowing Him to "come in".

Esther's destiny was a governmental position. We as a church redeemed by Christ are now kings and priests seated with Him in heavenly places (Rev 1:6, Eph 2:6-7). Kings and priests are governmental positions. When His Church is operating from a governmental seat of heaven, the enemies' plans are reversed, and justice is released.

Esther was a light to expose the wicked strategies of the enemy and release a nation from the decree of death.

And so, God is positioning His chosen/Church, a purified and prepared remnant, into strategic positions of influence, to thwart the enemies' plans and strategies.

POSITIONING FOR THE EXECUTION OF JUSTICE

In early June 2018, I had a dream regarding the number 9. I saw 999 repeatedly throughout my dream and as the number 9 repeatedly showed up I kept saying in my dream, "This is recompense, reconciliation and redemption". In the same dream I repeatedly saw 4:14 alongside 999. In the dream I was saying "this is now the time of Esther". I knew this meant Esther 4:14

> *For if you keep silent at this time, relief and deliverance shall arise for the Jews from elsewhere, but you and your father's house will perish. And who knows but that you have come to the kingdom for such a time as this and for this very occasion?*

The biblical meaning of the number 9 is "finality" or the "fullness" of God. The finality of God comes with a connotation of justice and judgement. We see that Jesus died on the cross on the 9th hour of the day. It was finished. This sacrifice was finalised on the 9th hour and what followed was redemption, reconciliation and recompense for all who would receive His sacrifice, both Jew and Gentile.

We also see that there are nine and nine fruits of the Spirit, which symbolise the "fullness" of God.

The Lord spoke to my heart regarding the interpretation saying :

"I am positioning my beloved as in Esther 4:14 for such a time as this, to execute My justice in this season (999), where I am bringing a finality to the cause of the enemy and turnaround for my people. Through this Esther government the plans of the enemy will be exposed on many levels in the seven mountains of society, and justice and finality will be brought as the

Lord's people lift up their voice and keep not silent. For with much given, much is required and with promotion comes responsibility."

THIS IS NOT THE TIME TO BE SILENT!

Notice in Esther 4:14, Mordecai is beseeching Esther *not* to keep silent. In order for justice to manifest, the voice of the Lord's beloved is to be heard. As she is heard, justice, recompense and redemption will come. God is calling a people who will not retreat in the face of the fear of what man can do to them! No, the Lord is positioning a people like Esther who will say, "If I perish, I perish" (Esther 4:16), and go forth in the fear of the Lord, seeing a mighty deliverance come (Psalm 34:7). As the Lord's people choose to not sit passively by in the council of the ungodly, but instead speak up and stand up, or repent for not doing so in the past (Psalm 1), we will begin to see divine turnarounds, recompenses, restitutions and unprecedented victories of advancement for the Kingdom of heaven.

The Lord is positioning His people in this hour to be a voice in the darkness, bringing finality to the wicked unjust plans of Haman!

PURIFICATION, BEAUTIFICATION, PRESENTATION, DEMONSTRATION

As Esther went through a purification and beautification process before she was presented to the king (Esther 2:12), the Lord also brings His people through a preparation season of purification to be able to operate successfully in the position of influence that He is promoting them to. The purification process serves the purpose of emptying out all agendas of the heart that aren't surrendered to the Lord. This process can take years, especially for positions of great influence. We see this in Joseph's life.

Like Esther, after this process of purifying and refining, the Lord beautifies His people with the fragrance of His favor causing them to be positioned for demonstration. Their preparation has come to its fullness (9) and now is the time for their positioning to demonstrate the kingdom for "such a time as this".

I have been seeing 007 (which to me symbolises secret agent assignments), in repeated fashion over a long time, reminding me of the Lord positioning His prepared ones for the execution of those assignments. The Lord is giving new assignments of justice in this new era and He is positioning His beloved to fulfil and execute those assignments.

Esther's assignment in a nutshell was an assignment of justice, exposing the evil plan of Haman (which was to annihilate the Jews) and bringing about a divine turnaround: her people gaining the right to defend themselves! She needed the favor of God to be chosen as queen and for her assignment to be fulfilled. And so, it is with God's people, those who have gone through the seasons of purification, fire, testings and trials and have come out purified, are now being beautified with the Lord's fragrance of favor to demonstrate His assignments of justice.

FRAGRANCE OF FAVOR FOR THE ASSIGNMENTS OF JUSTICE

In a time of intercession in the later part of 2018, I had a vision of the Lord spraying perfume all around Esther. I knew this represented his prepared people. I then saw a two-edged sword being wielded and the Lord giving it to His people. As He gave it to them, I heard Him say,

"This is a sword of FAVOR and VENGEANCE, for you will need favor in order to execute my righteous vengeance on the enemy in this season".

I knew this was a symbolic picture of His bride being Esther and the fragrance and perfume of His anointing to adorn her with favor, positioning her to fulfil her assignment and execute the justice of the Lord.

Esther's assignment reversed the decree from a death sentence to a preservation of life.

RESURRECTION POWER FOR THE LAID DOWN LOVERS

And they overcame him by the blood of the Lamb, and by the word of their testimony; and they loved not their lives unto the death (Revelation 12:11 KJV).

The verse clearly portrays the power to overcome is in loving not our lives even unto death. We touched on this notion earlier in this chapter, in reference to Esther facing death.

May I make the bold statement that the power of God that will cause great generational and national shifts and victories, is reserved for the laid down lovers of God.

Like Ester saved her nation from the decree of death, so this generation of laid down lovers who are carriers of the glory will overcome death as they die to themselves and walk in the resurrection power of God.

You can't bear resurrection life if you are already alive. Resurrection life comes on somebody who has died. For it is no longer I that lives but Christ that lives within me (Galatians 2:20).

To overcome, God will lead you in an unconventional way. There will always be risks or else it wouldn't require faith.

Ester exposed the strategies of evil to save a generation. She loved her life not even unto death to obey the Lord. And this same call is being heralded out of heaven now. Arise oh Esther, arise, My bride, My beloved, for have you not been called to the Kingdom for such a time as this!

Chapter 10

THE KISS OF HIS ROAR

Today as I am writing sixteen years after my encounter with the Lion of Judah in 2003 which I described in the first Chapter, I close this book with an unexpected encounter and visitation I had with the Lion of Judah just days ago.

ENCOUNTER WITH THE LION OF JUDAH

I was leading a women's meeting in worship and word, as I said, just days before I wrote the final chapter of this book, and the fire of the Lord fell so strong on me. This fire was filled with a love enveloped by fury as He began to speak to His beloved. When He spoke, it was as if He was roaring. His words were strong, filled with urgency, an urgency I had not yet experienced in all my years of ministering His word to His people.

This urgency apprehended me in an unapologetic type delivery that was for those with ears to hear what He was saying in this time.

After processing this encounter with the Lord, He spoke to me and said,

> *"for as I said in 2003 I am "coming as the Lion", know this day I have now come! I have come for those who have made themselves ready, I have come to those who have been seeking, I have come to those who have ears to hear and eyes to see, to roar over them and draw them into My chamber."*

He then began to speak to my heart concerning Song of Songs chapter 1:1-4. Let's feast verse by verse as He reveals His heart for His beloved.

LET HIM KISS YOU

> *Let Him kiss me with the kisses of his mouth: for thy love is better than wine (Song of Songs 1:2 KJV).*

According to Strong's Concordance, kiss in the Hebrew is *nashaq*, it is a primitive root with the idea *"to fasten upon"*.[1] This word is identical to the Hebrew word *nawsak*; which means to *catch fire/to kindle*.[2]

These words have a close correlation to the Hebrew word *chazaq*, which also means to fasten upon. In other words, meaning to *conquer or seize*.[3] This word *chazaq*, is the same Hebrew word used for "show Himself strong" in 2 Chronicles 15:7. *Chazaq* is also correlated to *chashaq* which means to: *delight in, to love, to join, to desire, but also to **deliver***.[4]

I wondered why the Shulamite woman in Song of Solomon first says, "*Let*" Him kiss me with the kisses of His mouth. It wasn't until I read the Hebrew meaning of the word kiss, that I began to understand this language.

She is speaking to her heart saying, "heart surrender to these kisses, *let* Him kiss me, desire these kisses of His mouth for His love is better than wine".

Wine is symbolic of the counterfeit intoxication the world has to offer. The counterfeit source that His beloved runs to, for comfort, joy, peace, fulfilment, love etc. Wine can provide all these temporary benefits in the moment but leaves us empty in the end. This is the world. We seek gratification by chasing mammon, relationships and success in order to find peace, joy and love, but it only satisfies us will temporarily. It will leave you with a heart "hangover" of grief and internal despair.

So, in light of the Hebrew meanings of the words explained, I believe this is the prayer of the Shulamite woman in her deep pursuit of her beloved,

"There is nothing like your love. "Kiss" me with the fire of your love, deliver and conquer my heart by Your deep desire for me, a love as strong as death. Show Yourself strong and avenge the enemies of my soul that have kept us apart and hindered our intimacy. I yield to the kisses of Your fire Lord, I say come and seize my heart as Yours and Yours alone! For I know this world has nothing to offer me, it is empty and futile and doesn't come close to Your love."

This same prayer of the Shulamite woman is being birthed in His beloved even now. And it is going up to the throne of heaven, pulling down the Avenger, the Lion, the Lover of our souls. This is what the Holy Spirit is groaning through His beloved to purify His bride, so the Spirit and the bride may say, "Come Lord Jesus, come".

HIS KISSES ARE HIS ROAR

Those who have been prepared and have had their hearts tilled and ploughed in the last season will hear the roar of the Lion in this season. For the roar of the Lion sounds different to the bleats of the Lamb. These "kisses" of His mouth are His roar, set to kindle and awaken His people's hearts to His love by fire. This roar is His word, going forth like fire calling His bride into a sanctification, and separateness unto Him. He is drawing her "out from among them" so He may avenge her. He will deliver her from whatever may seek to keep her spotted. He is roaring with fire to burn up those enemies of His love in her heart, and urgently calling her to "cut loose", through repentance, all attachments to the things of this world and ideologies that go with it. It's time to come up, it's time to come up, it's time to come up higher, to think as He thinks, and understand as He knows (Isaiah 55:9).

The fire of God separates, purifies, sanctifies and causes us to be spotless from the world.

When kissed by the fire of His love, it will bring a separation and sanctification. It will purify the spots that have been left by the world. He is marking His beloved with fire, the fire of His love, to truly stand out as a beacon of truth to the world.

ADORNING HIS BELOVED WITH A NEW PERFUMED FRAGRANCE

Vs 3:

Because of the savour of thy good ointments thy name is
as ointment poured forth, therefore do the virgins love you.

Ointment is a prophetic symbol of anointing oil. These ointments were filled with fragrance.

In very recent days, I had an encounter when leading worship in our church service. I kept hearing, *cinnamon, frankincense* and *myrrh*. The Lord had me singing this out over and over again. I knew He was anointing His beloved in this hour with new fragrances of His anointing.

Myrrh

As I was singing, I saw the picture of Song of Songs 5 where the Shulamite woman was lying on her bed after a hard day's work in the vineyard and dreamt of her beloved coming to her. But she was so tired that she didn't want to get up and dirty her feet to open the door for him. Finally, she arose only to find he had gone and left the door knob dripping with sweet scented myrrh.

In biblical times, myrrh was used as one of the ingredients in the Holy Anointing Oil and also as a perfume. This anointing oil was to sanctify and separate the temple, the utensils and the priests as holy unto the Lord (Exodus 30:22-30). We see the oil of myrrh used in Esther's six-month purification before she was presented to the King (Esther 2:12). It was also used to embalm and purify the dead for burial.

The oil of myrrh that dripped on the doorknob represents an anointing for separation, sanctification and purification. As the Shulamite arose and put her hand on the doorknob where her beloved had been, she was being marked by His coming. It was His desire to mark her as separate unto Him by His love and His alone.

The Lord was quickening my heart to understand that His "coming" isn't always at our convenience. It could be when we are exhausted from our labours in His vineyard. I feel it is an urgent message from the Lord in this hour to respond to Him when He comes. He requires a response from us, and it may require us to soil our feet in order to meet Him. Responding to His coming, might require us to leave our comfort zone, the comfortable bed of slumber. He is marking His beloved with myrrh in this hour, separating and sanctifying her unto Himself as His and His alone. A pure bride, unspotted from the world.

Frankincense

Frankincense is burned as an incense. Frankincense was one of the ingredients of the incense noted in Exodus 30:34-38, which was to be placed in front of the Ark of the Covenant within the Tent of Meeting in the Tabernacle. Incense when burned, has a perfumed fragrant aroma. It is symbolic of prayers and offerings that are pleasing to God. This aroma speaks of devoted worship unto the Lord, exuding as a beautiful fragrance in His nostrils. This fragrance is what will exude from His beloved bride as she comes into the chambers of intimacy and walks a life of devoted worship unto Him.

Cinnamon

Cinnamon was also an ingredient in the Holy Anointing Oil (Exodus 30:23). It also has the connotation of a fragrance that exudes being separate unto the Lord. It is a spice with a beautiful aroma. In biblical times, along with myrrh, it was used to anoint the bed of intimacy (Proverbs 7:17). Cinnamon is a love spice. It is a fragrance of love, intimacy and romance. Even though Proverbs 7:17 is referring to a forbidden intimacy, it is still nonetheless exposing a traditional custom of the day, that the bed of intimacy was anointed with fragrances and one of them being cinnamon.

All three fragrances mentioned above represent consecration unto the Lord. These beautiful perfumes are what the Lord is adorning His beloved with in this season. She is being embalmed in consecration unto Him, exuding the fragrance of her love to her King and His love to her. This fragrance on her will be smelled by the world and will cause those seeking truth to be drawn to the Father.

DRAW ME TO THE CHAMBER

Verse 4:

> *Draw me, we will run after thee: the king hath brought me into his chambers: we will be glad and rejoice in thee, we will remember thy love more than wine: the upright love thee.*

To draw is to call out, or to lead out. To call out into a new place. The Lord is calling His people to come out from among the world and be separate! (2 Corinthians 6:17) The Lord is calling us from the present place we are in, and to pursue Him into the chamber. We see here in verse 4 of Song of Solomon 2, that the destination is His chambers, the destination is intimacy and consecration in immense intoxication of His love.

When we run after Him, which is an intense pursuit of His heart, we will meet with this intense fire of His love. Hebrews 12:29 clearly describes our God as an all-consuming fire. This fire will separate, this fire will purify, this fire will sanctify, this fire will awaken, this fire will kindle a love we have not yet known, this fire will AVENGE our enemies and will prepare a bride ready for her KING.

Let Him kiss you, beloved. Allow the kisses of His roar to mark you as His and His alone. Allow the fire of His love to avenge your cause as you embrace the Lion of Judah who has come to show Himself strong.

CONCLUSION

In this day that burns like an oven, in this hour that the Lord is roaring over His beloved with the fire of His kisses, drawing her (the spotless one walking in the fear of the Lord) to Himself, may the Avenger be seen rising upon her with healing in His wings. May she now go forth as calves released from the stall and may all sorrow be turned into joy. May the Lion of Judah, the King of Glory, the Avenger be seen as light arising on His beloved as heaven responds to gross darkness filling the earth. May nations and kings come to this light. May justice and restitution be demonstrated as the righteous tread down that which is lawless, as ashes under the soles of their feet. May His Kingdom come, His will be done, on earth as it is in heaven (Malachi 4, Song of Songs 2, Isaiah 60, Matthew 6).

My prayer is that all who have read this book would come into a deeper understanding of the King of Glory as their Avenging Lover. The One Who has made and is making ready His people, to come to and move through them.

With much Love,

Anita Alexander

NOTES

ALL Strong's Concordance References are taken from:
Strong's Exhaustive Concordance of the Bible, by James Strong.
Print book. English. 2009. Updated edition. Peabody,
Massachusetts: Hendrickson Publishers.

Chapter 2
THE AVENGER

1. Hebrew word pawar (Strongs H6286)
2. Hebrew word bosheth (Strongs H1322)
3. Hebrew word boosh (Strongs H954).
4. Hebrew word ranan (Strongs H7442)
5. Hebrew word yarash (Strongs H3423)
6. Hebrew word chazaq (Strongs H2388)
7. Hebrew word shalem (Strongs H8003)
8. Hebrew word kabod (Strongs H3519)

Chapter 3
MAKE WAY FOR THE KING OF GLORY

1. Greek word kamelos (Strongs G2574), Hebrew origin, root word gamal (Strongs H1580)

Chapter 4
A CHANGE OF LANDSCAPE

1. Hebrew word gay (Strongs H1516)
2. Reference Psalm 23:4 Hebrew word valley; gay (Strongs H 1516)
3. Hebrew word gevah (Strongs H1466)
4. Hebrew word nasah (Strongs H5375)
5. Reference Isaiah 53:4, Hebrew word lift; nasa (Strongs H5375)
6. Greek word phos (Strongs G5457)

7. Hebrew word aqob (Strongs H6121)
8. Greek word strepho (Strongs G1294)
10. Merriam-Webster's Online Dictionary, s.v. "perverse" (accessed August 27, 2018)
11. www.blueletterbible.org, Olive tree reference to Israel study, Blue Letter Bible, 2019 www.blueletterbible.org/study/larkin/dt/29.cfm (accessed March 25, 2019).
12. Hebrew word rekes (Strongs H7406), rakas (Strongs H7405)
13. www.studylight.org word search for Hebrew word rekes (Strongs H7406), Study Light.Org, 2001-2019, www.studylight.org/lexicons/hebrew/7406.html (accessed August 28, 2018
14. www.blueletterbible.org, Dictionary and Word Search for Hebrew word rekes (Strongs7406), Blue Letter Bible, 2019 https://www.blueletterbible.org/lang/lexicon/lexicon.cfm?Strongs=H7406&t=KJV (accessed August 28, 2018)
15. Hebrew word biqah (Strongs H1237)
16. www.blueletterbible.org, Dictionary and Word Search for Hebrew word biqar (Strongs H1237), Blue Letter Bible, 2019 www.blueletterbible.org/lang/lexicon/lexicon.cfm?Strongs=H1237&t=KJV (accessed March 25, 2019)
17. Hebrew word baqa (Strongs H1234)
18. Reference Psalm 78:13, Hebrew word baqa (Strongs H1234)
19. Hebrew word sela (Strongs H5553)
20. www.behindthename.com, Search for name meaning "Victor", Mike Campbell, 1996-2019, https://www.behindthename.com/name/victor (accessed August 27, 2018)
21. www.ancestry.com, Search for the name meaning "Franken", Ancestry, 1997-2019, https://www.ancestry.com/nameorigin?surname=franken&geo_a=r&geo_s=us&geo_t=us&geo_v=2.0.0&o_xid=62916&o_lid=62916&o_sch=Partners_ (accessed August 27, 2018)
22. www.nameberry.com , Search for name meaning "Frank", Nameberry, 2019, https://nameberry.com/babyname/Frank_ (accessed August 27, 2018)
23. www.ancestry.com.au, Search for meaning of "Stein", Ancestry, 1997-2019, https://www.ancestry.com.au/name-origin?surname=stein_(accessed August 27, 2018)

Chapter 5
MAY I COME IN?

1. Hebrew word bo (Strongs H935)
2. Hebrew word darash (Strongs H1875)
3. Hebrew word baqash (Strongs H1245)
4. www.studylight.org, Dictionary and Word Search for Hebrew word baqash (Strongs H1245), StudyLight.org , 2001-2019, https://www.studylight.org/lexicons/hebrew/1245.html (accessed August, 28 2018)
5. Hebrew word naw-saw (Strongs H5375)
6. Hebrew word rosh (Strongs H7218)
7. Hebrew word shaar (Strongs H8179)
8. www.studylight.org Dictionary and Word Search of Hebrew word shaar (Strongs H8179), StudyLight.org, 2001-2019, https://www.studylight.org/lexicons/hebrew/8179.html (accessed March 25, 2019)
9. Hebrew word owlam (Stongs H5769)

Chapter 6
THE DISMANTLING OF FALSE HEADS

1. Greek word antichristos (Strongs G500)
2. www.studylight.org, Dictionary and Word Search for "wrestle", (Strongs G3823), StudyLight.org, 2001-2019, www.studylight.org/lexicons/greek/3823.html (accessed January 15, 2019)
3. English Oxford online Dictionary, s.v "politics", Oxford University Press, 2019, https://en.oxforddictionaries.com/definition/politics (accessed March 25, 2019)
4. www.lovesickscribe.com, Article, "A church without apology", Author, Dawn Hill (accessed January 2019).

Chapter 8
THE DAVIDIC GOVERNMENT

1. www.worthychristianforums.com/topic/96593-king-saul-and-repentance/ (accessed June 2018)

Chapter 10
THE KISS OF HIS ROAR

1. Hebrew word nashaq (Strongs H5401)
2. Hebrew word nawsak (Strongs H5400)
3. Hebrew word chazaq (Strongs H2388)
4. Hebrew word chashaq (Strongs H2836)

KINGDOM ACADEMY

*Raising up an Army
of Revolutionaries*

For more information about our
Ministry School of the Supernatural, go to:

www.revival-flame.org

Made in the USA
Columbia, SC
30 April 2019